MAXIMIZIN

Also available from Cassell:

Forsyth: *Career Skills*
Jones (ed.): *Introduction to Hospitality Operations*
Jones and Lockwood: *The Management of Hotel Operations*
Maitland: *The Small Business Marketing Handbook*
O'Connor: *Using Computers in Hospitality*
Walker, Ferguson and Denvir: *Creating New Clients*

Maximizing Hospitality Sales

How to sell hotels, venues and conference centres

Patrick Forsyth

CASSELL

Cassell
Wellington House, 125 Strand, London WC2R 0BB
370 Lexington Avenue, New York, NY 10017-6550

www.cassell.co.uk

First published 1999

British Library Cataloguing-in-Publication Data
A catalogue record for this book is available from the British Library.

ISBN 0-304-70428-8

Designed and typeset by Kenneth Burnley, Wirral, Cheshire
Printed and bound in Great Britain by
Biddles Ltd, Guildford and King's Lynn

Contents

'Mankind is divided into two great classes: hosts and guests.'

Sir Max Beerbohm

About the author

PATRICK FORSYTH is a Partner of Touchstone Training & Consultancy in London. His firm specializes in consultancy and training and the origination of training materials in marketing, sales and communications skills. A consultant for more than twenty years, he began his career in publishing and now works across a wide range of industries and in a number of different parts of the world; he conducts both in-company and public training programmes.

He has worked regularly with the hospitality industry. With airlines, hotels – both groups, such as InterContinental, Hilton and Holiday Inn, and independent properties – conference centres, travel agents and others in the UK, Europe and South East Asia. He has worked for professional bodies in the field including the Meetings Industry Association and the Singapore Hotels Association.

He is the author of a number of successful business books. These include: *How to be Better at Writing Reports and Proposals* (Kogan Page), *Making Successful Presentations* (Sheldon Press), *Career Skills: A Guide for Long-term Success* (Cassell) and *First Things First* – on time management (Pitman). In addition, he regularly writes articles for various business journals on aspects of sales and marketing.

Gill Smillie, who wrote the Foreword to this book, is Hon. Secretary to the Meetings Industry Association.

Gill founded and runs Conference Venues CountryWide, one of the UK's most respected venue-booking agencies which specializes in handling training meeting accommodation.

She has a background in the sales side of the industry, working successively for Centre Hotels, THF, Metropole Group and Grand Metropolitan. In a career now covering 25 years, Gill has been involved in most aspects of hospitality sales, particularly conference and banqueting.

As a venue finder, dealing with hundreds of venues on a daily basis, she is both critical of the performance of some sales staff, but at the same time delighted that management now appreciates how vital professionalism – and thus training – is as a means of raising standards of performance to help the industry grow and prosper.

Foreword

THE hospitality industry is widespread and of considerable financial importance to every economy in which it operates. It incorporates a whole range of properties, not just hotels but conference and training centres of all sorts, and a host of specialist venues, residential and non-residential, catering for guests on business or pleasure; and its size defies the imagination. Tens – perhaps hundreds of thousands – of people use these establishments every day, singly or in groups, on business or for pleasure, or a combination of both.

It is a challenging business, and neither finding nor catering for its many customers is an easy matter: more so in the volatile market conditions at the turn of a new millennium. What is necessary to succeed and do so profitably in a way that guarantees growth and development in the future can be summed up in one word: excellence. Excellence of facilities, equipment, advice, arrangements and service; and all made possible by one thing – people. Without excellence in these areas little progress will be possible.

In every aspect of the hospitality industry the customers want good service. Without this they will not do business with us – or, if they do, there will be no chance of their returning. In a service business this is obvious enough, but what exactly do customers mean by 'good service'? Whatever else they may mean – and it is a phrase that will encompass a great deal – they want to be dealt with by people in the industry in the right way; and that means in a way that recognizes that without customers there would be no business. And they want the role of the people to be excellent throughout the whole process of doing business with us: not just during their stay or visit, but before and after as well. Sales staff, to whom this book is primarily directed, are involved at every stage, and for many customers represent their first point of contact with us. If they do not get their part right, any potential business relationship will be stillborn.

To achieve the order of excellence which customers demand means the industry must field staff who understand their role and whose expertise to execute their tasks is finely developed. This will not just happen: it is dependent on careful recruitment and selection, on briefing and ongoing development and, of course, on good management.

Instilling the right skills and making them practical and appropriate in every area is vital; so too is maintaining them. This is perhaps especially important in the sales area (that is not to underrate any other category of staff, but unless sales bring in the business there will be no customers requiring service). And, in an industry not renowned for its investment in training, every practical aid to stimulate the process is to be welcomed.

So I am pleased to be associated with the publication of this book. The author is one of those who has worked with the UK's Meeting Industry Association, who have a mission to raise standards and use their activities as part of their regular work to achieve this aim, to help promote the need for excellence, and assist the move towards it.

From this I know his work is practical, and this volume sets out some of his views and advice on how to maximize the effectiveness of selling in this area. It is not possible to write a book by committee, much less to involve the members of a whole association or industry, so the content is ultimately his. I personally find much to agree with here, and hope that the book's publication will act as one more catalyst to the process of making an already successful industry still better able to compete in the modern competitive and dynamic world.

GILL SMILLIE
Hon. Secretary, The Meetings Association

Preface

'I am the world's worst salesman: Therefore I must make it easy for people to buy.'

F. W. Woolworth

Offering hospitality – a unique commercial challenge

People elect to stay in hotels for a host of reasons. A stay may involve one person staying one night or 200 delegates attending a residential conference for a full week and utilizing bedrooms, meeting rooms, restaurants and every other hotel facility. Guests may come from near or far, from the same country or overseas, singly or in groups, on business or for social reasons. Sometimes they *want* to visit the hotel – it is a treat, like a holiday or a weekend break; sometimes they would much rather be at home and only the necessities of business or the unpleasantness of some crisis demand that they spend time in a hotel. Similar kinds of circumstance are attendant on the use of a range of venues within the overall hospitality business: a conference centre or residential training centre for instance. The permutations are almost endless.

But, in every case, a decision has to be made. People must consider: Do they use a hotel at all? Can the meeting be run in the boardroom or must they go outside? Can they afford a holiday? And if outside accommodation is going to be the order of the day, the question moves on to consider which, of a number of possibilities, they will select. Often such judgements are finely balanced. A particular venue may well be chosen not because it is radically different from another, but because of some small but significant difference that swings the decision in its favour.

Those running the business must ensure that sufficient decisions of this sort are made in their favour daily to produce the desired commercial results. A hotel or venue has to be marketed just like any other product, as a service business in every sense of the word. The people, and the services they deliver, are just as important as the facilities – perhaps more so. One of the prime characteristics of any service business is that what they offer to the market cannot be kept in stock. When an airplane takes off, any unsold seat represents revenue and profit gone for ever, similarly an empty bedroom, an unused meeting-room, or too few people in a restaurant on a particular day, also represent an opportunity that can never be recouped. So the process of bringing in customers – 365 days every year – is relentless.

Bringing in the business

Consider what is involved in achieving this. The marketing process spans the whole business activity. It must identify any need that exists, it is involved in research and in planning and, above all, in promotion. Marketing is a concept which demands that the focus of the business is on the customer and so, in a service business, this is also linked inextricably to the whole area of customer service and the staff who deliver it. In any venue, service is, of course, paramount. Yet delivering first-class service to every customer every time is by no means easy.

Some years ago, an apocryphal story was reported in the *Financial Times*. It concerned a senior executive of a major American hotel chain staying in the London hotel of the group for a few days and being less than impressed with the service he received. Finally at breakfast on the third morning he could stand it no longer. He introduced himself to the waitress who served him and explained that as a senior Vice-President of the hotel he had to tell her something about the service she must provide: 'Everyone who comes into the restaurant should not only get good food,' he said, 'but a kind word and a pleasant smile.' Suitably chastened she disappeared and returned a few minutes later with a plate of eggs and bacon. He looked up at her and was rewarded with a thin smile. 'Better,' he said, 'but what about the kind word?' To which she replied without hesitation: 'I recommend you don't eat the eggs!'

It may seem unfair, but as the saying goes, 'The customer is king' and this is realistically the way business works. Getting service right goes with the territory. This is the background against which marketing has to operate. If we look in detail at the promotional activity involved, we find a number of stages. Assume someone who has never heard of your own property. Initially, they may become aware of it in a number of ways. They may see an advertisement; read a brochure; see some editorial mention (inspired by public relations activity); receive a recommendation from a past user; meet you at a function or exhibition; or simply know the venue (they drive past it on their way to work or are invited to a lunch at the venue). All these – and more, as part of a carefully planned and implemented promotional strategy – may play a part in creating awareness. This can produce business with no further action being necessary. In other words, some business may arrive from customers who have no more than an awareness of your existence. A businessman, or his secretary, may well telephone to book an overnight stay on the basis of a mere entry in some directory and the information that you are within a mile of a particular road junction or in a certain part of a city.

Other kinds of business are seen by the prospective customer as requiring more information. They will not just make a booking, other stages have to be gone through – the customer sees this as checking you out and you will doubtless regard it as a sales opportunity. It is the same for many kinds of customer and many kinds of usage of the hotel. For example, the process is not so dissimilar for someone contemplating where to book a wedding reception or a businessman wanting to accommodate a company meeting of some sort. Promotion prompts interest – 'Tell me more' – and sales has to convert that initial interest into firm business, a process that can take a number of meetings or other contacts and last over weeks or months. However, if promotion cannot prompt sufficient enquiries, then the sales department must take an initiative to create some of the new interest itself, and prospecting is then part of the job. And, because repeat business is so important, the development of existing customers is also vital.

None of this just happens. Even the best property will not sell itself. Yet often sales approaches can include the assumption that the place speaks for itself. For example, if I go to a hotel or similar venue to check out the facilities for a training event, then I have specific things in mind: about the event, the people attending, the atmosphere, and the necessary physical requirements. Over the years, I have very often found that the salesperson has a very standardized approach. They give you the set patter about the place, they take you around the so-called 'show-round' – on what I call automatic pilot – and generally the feeling you get is that the whole thing is little tailored to you or to your needs. This feeling is confirmed by many other users to whom I speak. As a result, when things are really well done the approach is sure to stand out; something that is an important element of differentiation in an industry where customers see many venues as essentially similar. How do you ensure this happens?

Customers are individuals. They are unique and like to be treated as such by the salespeople with whom they deal. And the hospitality business is different from other types of business: it is special, and is not like selling motor cars or computers. It is a service. Services by their nature cannot be tested in advance, so those who come to you for the first time, with no prior experience of how your property operates, will want reassurance that all will go well 'on the day'. As the first person they may meet is likely to be in sales, not only does the sales process have to be persuasive, it must itself give signs of the good service that is to come. Literally, the first chance you get to impress people with your establishment's service is often while you sell to them. So the selling process has to be pitched very carefully. It has to differentiate your property from the others – sometimes many others – that may provide ready alternatives to the services which you offer.

Selling in this business depends on sound knowledge of the property and all its facilities; a similarly thorough understanding of clients and customers, who they are, what they need, how they think; and an understanding of the sales techniques that work best in this specialized field and the ability to deploy them appropriately day by day, customer by customer, and meeting by meeting.

This is what this book reviews, starting with some of the overall issues and the way you should view the activity. Thereafter it develops broadly chronologically, starting with the need to find and contact new prospects and then looking in detail at the nature of the typical face-to-face contacts that occur with them (including the classic 'show-round') and, because repeat business is something everyone wants, the ongoing process of customer development and management.

The aim is to look specifically at the nature of selling in the context of the special nature of this industry. So it is intended specifically for those on the sales side, for their managers; for them it adopts a practical, 'How-to' approach. It is as much for those with some experience, who wish to review and improve the way they work, as for newcomers to the field. It is also for those going into the industry who need to appreciate how this side of the business should operate (and some of whom may ultimately get involved in it); many in this latter group may be students, for whom it will be useful reading. I draw on a variety of experiences and on the knowledge of many people I have met in the industry over the years (see the Acknowledgements). In addition, I intentionally take the role of devil's advocate on some issues to project the view of the customer or client.

One final point is important as we set out on this review. That is the fragile nature of the sales process. By this I mean the distinct possibility that small details and small differences in the way selling is approached make a disproportionate difference to the outcome. The difference between a prospect saying they will book, or not, may literally depend on the choice of one word in the discussion rather than another. Certainly, such differences may seem minimal at the time: one additional question asked, a more descriptive turn of phrase, a little more preparation or trouble taken over some arrangement can make a difference. This is doubly true if a prospect is checking you out alongside one or more of your competitors and making comparisons as they go; and usually, of course, they are doing exactly that. They compare establishments and facilities, and more; but they also compare the people they met and how things were done. You never know which points may potentially make a real difference to the approach you take. The only option is to ensure everything you do is appropriate to each individual prospect or customer with whom you deal. Examples of some of these factors are given throughout the book.

There is a great deal hanging on all this. Even a small venue has challenging targets, and the difference between being 60 per cent booked and, say, 90 per cent booked represents a significant change in profitability. Do not be deceived by percentages, by the way. Ninety per cent occupancy may sound good – indeed for many it is good – but percentages can disguise the real figures on which we should concentrate. For example, in a 400-bedroom hotel, 90 per cent full still means the profit from 40 rooms is being lost. If this was the case all through the year, then the number of lost rooms is 40×365 which is 14,600; that represents a very great deal of revenue and illustrates dramatically something of what is to be gained from getting the sales effort right. And the overall objective of everything we discuss here is just that: maximizing the effectiveness of what is done through the sales side of the business, to hit profitable sales that will hit targets.

PATRICK FORSYTH
Touchstone Training & Consultancy
28 Salcote Maltings, Heybridge, Essex CM9 4QP

Acknowledgements

A NY consultant is in a privileged position. They get to see many different businesses from the inside, and with some they get involved and are able to play a part in helping them become more successful. Yet they never know quite as much about the nature of the businesses they work with as those who manage them, and in technical businesses the gap is larger. With some clients, however, I have always felt that there is a greater bond – when I am also a client or customer of their business. This is certainly true of the world of hotels and venues.

Over the years of working as a trainer and consultant I have stayed and worked in more hotels than I care to remember. Sometimes, the stay has been overnight. At other times, I have stayed for a week or more, occasionally without emerging from a meeting room at all during the stay except to eat or sleep. Sometimes the hotel's standard of service lingers in my memory long after the stay. On other occasions, the mind mercifully blots out the whole unfortunate experience in moments, save for a firm mental note exclaiming 'Never, ever again!' A few become firm favourites, old friends to which one readily returns.

In addition to staying and working in hotels on business, and occasionally on holiday, I have worked for numerous organizations in the hotel and venue business, as well as related areas in the broader travel industry. These have ranged from major international groups to small independent hotels, and have included residential and non-residential conference and meeting providers of all sorts. My experience in this respect has included work – mainly in-company and public seminars – in the UK, in

Europe and in South East Asia. My work has also, in recent years, involved me on occasion with the Meetings Industry Association (MIA): such included a period as its Training Adviser and additionally the public seminars on marketing and sales matters I have conducted for them over time.

Two MIA training packages are mentioned, indeed drawn on, within the book. I was involved in writing the material for them and, in one case, with the accompanying video. Both may be useful to readers of this text: *Comprehending Clients* and *Meeting on Good Terms* which look at identifying and using client needs and arranging the terms and conditions of the contractual arrangements involved in sales through workbooks and video.*

Through all of this I have met many more people from this fascinating business, and I have drawn on all of this background and experience for this book. So, I am grateful to all I have met along the way, as a customer or a trainer, and have learned a great deal from the experiences they shared wittingly or otherwise.

In addition, I would like to thank all those who have made specific comments (some of which are quoted and acknowledged) and would mention particularly Tim Chudley, who runs a well-known, and rightly highly regarded residential conference centre, Highgate House. Though I know he did not have time to read the manuscript, he did so anyway, looking at and commenting on an early draft, and I am grateful for the most useful feedback he provided.

Finally, thanks are due to Gill Smillie who kindly agreed amongst her many duties to write the Foreword to this book; I am grateful for that and for the many areas of this fascinating business she has led me into over the years.

PATRICK FORSYTH, 1998

---

* Details of these are available from the Meetings Industry Association, 34 High Street, Broadway, Worcs WR12 7DT.

Dedicated to Gill:

A good friend, and invaluable guide and guru to a fascinating industry.

1 Complex, competitive and hard work: an introduction

WORKING in hospitality sales for a hotel or venue places you in a key role in one of the most exciting and challenging industries that exist. It is international in extent, already very big business and, in most markets, it seems to have a considerable long-term growth potential. What does this make it like to work in?

First, consider the good news. The service nature of the business makes it potentially very satisfying. Your customers come to you, so assuming you are based at your venue (some people will be elsewhere, at group office for instance, though no doubt visiting regularly), you are close to their use of the venue. When it goes well you know about it – and, of course, when it does not. You have, in part, an advisory role. You are in the business of helping ensure that a multiplicity of client arrangements goes well. The scale varies too – from a simple overnight stay or weekend break for one or two people, to a major conference for two hundred – as do the kinds of people you deal with. For the most part, no two days are the same: there is variety and a new challenge every day. In addition, there is a considerable personal autonomy; when things go well it may be not just because you saw it on its way, but because of an initiative you took, then seeing it right through. Teamwork is important too, and the jobs involved often necessitate a flexible working together rather than rigid dividing lines. At best it is rewarding and fun.

But the task of filling a hotel, or any other kind of venue, consistently in all departments 365 days every year is not an easy one. It is challenging, and more so than ever before in today's competitive markets, and those of the new millennium. In many a sales department, people would regard resources, time and backup services as stretched rather than in abundance. Operational matters sometimes intrude, with salespeople sometimes taking their turn as duty manager.

None of this makes it easy. It can also be frustrating: patience is necessary to see things through, as is attention to detail to ensure good services. It is a professional task which circumstances can make difficult to execute in a professional way. Yet professionalism is what customers demand.

But, overall, the balance appears to be positive, the problems are not insurmountable and the satisfactions are obtainable. Many people spend a lifetime in the industry and find it difficult to imagine working in any other field. From the sales point of view, it is not so different from any other business – it depends on sufficient people booking sufficient services and paying enough for them to produce the targeted return. Further, it depends on many of these people or organizations being sufficiently pleased with the experience to come back, or being persuaded to come back, for more. The nature of the business makes the sales job a very particular one. It is relentless and not at all like dealing with a commodity that can be held in stock. A property has to be put over to prospective customers in such a way that it is differentiated from the competition, seems attractive and convinces people of the good service to come. Selling hotels is not like selling toothpaste or ball bearings.

This book sets out to review the techniques involved and show what makes for an effective approach in this industry and what helps with the important process of differentiating your property from others. It investigates the overall process, because the way in which you go about it and the structure you bring to bear is important. It reviews the sequence of events and the different kinds of meetings involved, and looks also at important details along the way. Often, what makes the difference between a 'Yes' and a 'No' is seemingly a detail, a difference of word or phrase, of question asked or not, of clarity of description or recognition of a customer need.

We start by reviewing some of the overall factors that are

involved, factors which, if you keep them firmly in mind, can help you adopt the right kind of approach more certainly, prompting better results. Consider first the most basic question: Why should people use hotels at all?

Why use outside facilities?

Hotels meet two basic needs. First, they provide facilities for the body to 'recharge its batteries' – food, drink, sleep and relaxation or leisure pursuit. Secondly, they provide space and facilities to carry out group activities for which there are no comparable or appropriate equivalent on company premises or at home. In both cases, either business or social factors can give rise to the need. The chart in Figure 1.1 makes this clear, illustrating four kinds of use.

	Business	
Social/pleasure	'Recharge'	Group activities

Figure 1.1: Basic needs met by hotels

In both cases such use should be regarded as optional. For instance, a business person may decide that a long journey home, albeit arriving late, is better than another night in a hotel. A company may decide to save money by squeezing a meeting into their own facilities despite this being less than ideal – or they may increase the budget and take a conference overseas. Similarly, a wedding may be held in the village hall or a 'Thank you' lunch be held at home. Even when a decision has been taken to go outside, then a further decision is involved in deciding where precisely to go; this is the competition that has already been mentioned, and in most situations the customer has plenty of choice.

It is sometimes sobering to curtail your enthusiasm and keep in mind that, while superficially your customers may seem to draw some pleasure from using the hotel, they may, in fact, very much prefer to be elsewhere. A host of reasons may be involved, ranging from a difficult journey to too much time away from home or base and perhaps the missing of particular events such as a birthday or important meeting. The good service and facilities they expect are sometimes regarded as compensation for what they would rather have. Of course, the reverse of all this is sometimes true too. Going to a hotel is an event, a treat and something pleasurable to which to look forward; this is true of a range of circumstances, from a family outing to a motivational business event. This realistic view is the foundation we will return to unashamedly in a number of ways. Seeing things from the customers' point of view will help you do better at everything in the sales process.

Sources of contact

Keep in mind the various sources of your contact with people. How they come to talk with you will affect their thinking, their view of you, their image of the property, how much they feel they already know about the place and how well it will meet their requirements; and thus, in turn, you will know how to deal with them.

They may:

- be past, or regular, users;
- be in receipt of a recommendation about you from a past user;
- be responding to some kind of promotion;
- be in touch with another part of the organization (e.g. another hotel in a group);
- have looked you up in a directory;
- be someone you are cold calling/prospecting;
- contact you via an intermediary (e.g. a conference booking agency or travel agent);
- simply have seen the hotel, perhaps from the car on a journey.

In each case, they will have a different perspective on the property, a different base and quantity of information about it – ranging from a thorough knowledge to none at all. And in each case they will expect to be dealt with specially. Taking this concept further, it is worth noting where contacts come from and how many come from each source. This can be represented as a percentage of the total and in the form of a pie chart (see Figure 1.2).

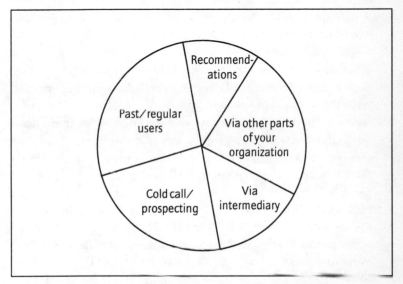

Figure 1.2: Percentage of business from various sources

This kind of analysis helps plan sales activities. Some of the categories may be self-generating, with a similar regular number of contacts tending to come from other group hotels, for example. Others may be more in the marketing area: it must be decided how many enquiries promotional activity must prompt. In still other categories, sales may need to initiate activity to produce a number of contacts that will increase the revenue from those areas, which are more self-generating, and bring it up to target. (There is more about prospecting in Chapter 3.) We now turn to the way in which customers choose one place over another.

Criteria for choice

By and large, customer choice is not a simple matter: a whole range of factors is assessed to ascertain which option they will pursue, and it is the perceived mix of these which swings them one way or another, towards venue A or B. Customers want answers to a whole list of questions; some of these they ask, others they discover from simply looking around the venue or flicking through its brochure. Some of these factors are tangible, some are intangible, and certainly customers rate some as major and others as peripheral.

Such factors include:

- availability (they can only book if you have the capacity they want at the time they want it);
- location (both geographically, and in terms of the immediate surroundings – town; country; scenery; shops; etc.);
- facilities (size; choice of restaurants; range of recreational facilities; telecommunication facilities; charges; etc.);
- service (remembering your customer's name; time taken to check in and out; room service and service at food and beverage outlets and the business centre);
- atmosphere (ambience; decor; upkeep of facilities and surroundings);
- price (people want 'value for money').

Amongst all these there are sometimes *cut-in* points; i.e., a customer will say to themselves that they will short-list or consider somewhere that has a nice pool or a 24-hour coffee shop. Similarly they take a view of other factors in a negative way – a *cut-out* – saying they will not consider anywhere without, say, a car park. Because hotels are often, from the clients' perspective, very similar in facilities and services, if not so much in looks, an objective analysis of two or more competing properties may not distinguish between them. They both seem to have the same standard of room, are similarly priced, have much the same range of services – what does the undecided customer do then? They fall back on intangible, or frankly peripheral points. They pick the one that has the nicest appearance, that provides transport to the station or airport, that has in-house movies, or where the salesperson seems to understand them best, is most immediately efficient or just more persuasive. On many occasions, what sways the business one way or another may seem ridiculously minor, but minor points often help customers to decide. In fact, customers want to be able to justify their decision to themselves and, in an organization, perhaps also to others. Which brings us to another point worth bearing in mind.

Buying motivation

Many buyers represent a company or organization of some sort. If so, they tend to represent two points of view in parallel. They act in a personal way, choosing a hotel according to their own preference and comfort, even in a way that reduces the effectiveness to the organization. At the same time, they are concerned for the company, something that often involves them worrying about what other, perhaps more senior, people will think of any decision they make and the arrangements that go with it.

Such motivation becomes very particular in any individual case. In booking a meeting room, a buyer may be thinking of the meeting as much as the facilities it requires. What happens at the meeting may be important to reputations, to getting the right decision made financially; or it may have very personal implications for someone's career or comfort. This links to the content of the next chapter which is concerned with the detail of understanding the customer's point of view.

As well as bearing in mind the buyer's motivation, it is important to understand and work with the way in which the buyer goes through a decision-making process. If you under-stand something of the psychology of what is taking place, there is a much greater chance that what you do can be matched to it and that the buyer will see your actions as appropriate rather than aggressive. Remember that the image of salespeople is not necessarily perfect and that people do not necessarily welcome those wearing a sales hat.

How people buy

The best and simplest definition of selling I have ever heard is that selling is helping people to buy. It is also accurate. The old-style image of selling as something you do to people is outmoded, as is advice about how to sell, which commends an approach which unthinkingly proceeds by rote.

Selling is better thought of as something you do *with* people. It must consciously be related to the individual buyer in a way that ensures acceptance, removes suspicion and builds trust. Think of your best customer or your oldest client – there is almost certainly not just rapport and respect between two professionals, there is trust too, and often contact may be initiated very much in terms of seeking advice: 'We are thinking of changing the format of this year's conference, do you think . . .' The best salespeople set out to create this kind of interaction and to do so promptly and certainly.

Selling works best when it proceeds in parallel with the way buying decisions are made and the thinking that it involves. Classically, using an approach first formalized by psychologists in the US, this thinking goes through seven stages:

1 'I am important and I want to be respected.'
2 'Consider my needs.'
3 'How will your ideas help me?'
4 'What are the facts?'
5 'What are the snags?'
6 'What shall I do?'
7 'I approve (or not).'

This seems like common sense; indeed if you think about it, you will find it is what you do yourself in many everyday situations. A good analogy is that of 'weighing up' the case or argument, putting all the good points on one side, all the rest on the other and assessing the net effect. Any attempt that responds unsatisfactorily to any of these stages is unlikely to end in agreement. The buyer's mind has to be satisfied on each point before moving to the next, and to be successful, the persuading sequence must match this decision-making sequence, and run parallel to it.

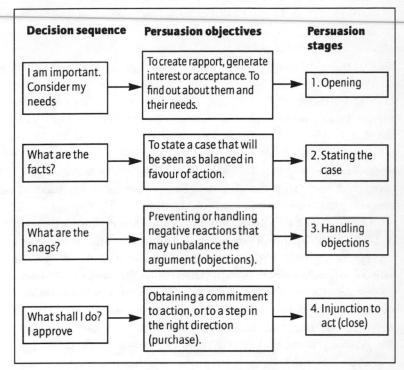

Figure 1.3: Decision-making process

Figure 1.3 shows the process alongside the persuasive objectives, what you are trying to achieve at each stage and the technique employed in any communication. The two keys to success are the process of matching the other person's progression and describing, selectively, your case, and discussing it in a way that relates to the circumstances of the other person.

The four main stages identified in the figure on the sales side are used to review the face-to-face meetings in Chapter 5. When persuasion works, both parties will have gone through this sequence stage by stage. However, if the attempt to persuade is unsuccessful, it will often be found that:

- the sequence has not taken place at all;
- some stage has been missed out;
- the sequence has been followed too quickly or too slowly, which means the salesperson is at one stage when the prospect wants to be, and expects the salesperson to be, at another. The two processes must proceed in tandem.

Early on, because people may well need to go through a number of stages – they may want proposals in writing, to confer with a colleague or actually look round a particular venue – you may not always be able to aim immediately for a commitment to buy. You must, however, have some other, clear objective on which to get a commitment. A positive 'Yes' to your putting in a written proposal is a good step in the right direction. The persuasion of what you are doing throughout the process must be lined up towards such an end.

Imagine, as a simple example, that a secretary wants the boss to buy a new word processor. The ultimate objective is for them to say 'Yes, buy it' about a particular machine. But it may be a step in the right direction to get them to review some brochures, check the quality of the present machine, have a demonstration, get a quote and so on. Sometimes there are many steps to go through before the ultimate objective can be achieved. Progressing through each, like taking steps up a ladder, is significant in reaching the end point, whether it is the top of the ladder or the objective we have set.

In hospitality selling, there may be a need to move to and then past interim objectives, to send details in writing, to visit the client, to get them to visit you and see the property and so on. Whatever your objective is, however, it is important to know and to be able to recognize the various stages ahead. With any individual contact you can identify the following:

- What stage has been reached in the decision process?
- Whether your sequence matches it.
- If not, why not?
- What do you need to do if the sequence does not match?
- Has a step been missed?

- Are you going too fast?
- Should you go back in the sequence?
- Can your objectives still be achieved, or were they the wrong objectives?
- How can you help the other person through the rest of the buying process?

Naturally, the whole process is not always covered in only one contact between salesperson and prospect; several meetings or exchanges may be necessary.

With this in mind as a sound foundation to the thinking necessary to deploy an effective sales approach, we will move on. It has already been indicated that understanding the customer or client is basic to any attempt to persuade them to a course of action. This is the topic of Chapter 2. Thereafter we review the methods involved in ensuring that there is a sufficient number of people to attempt to understand and meet with, and in Chapter 3 we review the techniques of both prospecting and identifying potential new contacts and look at how best to make initial contact with them. Then, before moving on to the actual sales meeting, we review sequentially what preparation is necessary to the sales process and the positioning of the salesperson which is most likely to find favour with the customer. The face-to-face meeting is reviewed in Chapter 5, and some thoughts about a key part of this in the hotels and venues business – the so called show-round – are dealt with, before moving on to look at the longer-term management of clients aimed at producing repeat business and implementation.

Throughout the process, the factors touched on here and in the Preface are borne in mind. Selling venues, hotels, or any kind of conference facility, demands a special kind of sales approach, and because of the great variety of customers and circumstances it routinely involves, the successful salesperson needs to have the 'mechanics' of sales technique well buttoned-down. In other words, the mind must be free to direct the process and decide the precise way forward, something that is difficult if you are having to focus on some basic element such as the best way to describe some particular aspect of the property. Not so long ago I asked the sales executive with whom I was discussing the merits of their London property: 'What's the difference between your Standard rooms and the Executive ones?' The answer came back without hesitation: '£25.' I have heard such an answer many times before, yet this is surely not the answer. Not only must there be something better and more appropriate to say, but that something – or better still a variety of somethings – should have been ready to be said. If you have in mind the best way to describe the different styles and facilities of the two room types, then the mind can be a step ahead in planning how best to make the point to this particular client and what to follow it with also. Not least, such an approach helps the important task of differentiating one property from another.

Selling, at least in its component parts and individual techniques, is for the most part pretty much common sense. That is, the practical approaches do seem logical once identified. Any complexity is primarily in the orchestration of the whole process and in getting the detail exactly right; the successful salesperson has to keep a number of balls in the air at once and still keep going in the right direction – towards agreement to buy.

Both dealing with the basics and organizing the whole process demand skill and the considered use of the right mix of techniques; but if this was totally simple, it would not be so satisfying to get it right.

2 | Understanding the customer and positioning the sales approach

THERE IS nothing more important in the hospitality business than customers, clients and guests. Unlike some other industries where sales are directed at one specific category of customer, in the venues business salespeople can find themselves selling to a great variety of customer types. They vary by business function – from a marketing person to a training or personnel manager – and hierarchically – contact may be with anyone, from a secretary to a managing director. The nature of their business varies; from a small local business to a large multinational corporation – with the area of business in which they are potentially interested varying too; overnight accommodation, a day meeting, a social event or a residential conference.

But they all have two things in common. First, they are demanding, they put their own position first, doing business only when their needs are met; at worst, they can be difficult, sometimes rude and always fickle. Secondly, they expect you to understand their position, their requirements, their business and circumstances and their needs. If they want you to accommodate a meeting, for example, they see your role as helping their meeting go well, not simply as being a provider of standard facilities and services.

It is a demanding role for those doing the selling. They have to be able to sell the range of services and facilities their property provides to a wide range of different people in differing circumstances and do so in each case in a way that is seen as individually appropriate by the prospect.

What are the implications here for the salesperson? While the whole process of selling in all its component detail must reflect the clients' point of view, here we focus on two key issues – the positioning of the sales role, and the need to understand clients and their requirements.

Sales approach and manner

It has already been said that, in a service business, the customer – unable to test the 'product' – relies heavily on any indication of how things will be, and such indications come through the salespeople who see the customer first. Of course, an intending client considering whether to place major business may decide to book himself in for a night's stay or for dinner with his wife, and this would constitute a fair test.

This is exactly the scenario in the excellent Video Arts training video entitled *Welcome Customer*, in which a customer is seen checking in and experiencing the less-than-good services throughout a particular hotel – Reception, Room Service, Maintenance, Restaurant, etc. – and only as he leaves, with the damage of poor service done so that he is unlikely ever to return, does it become clear that his stay was for the sole purpose of checking whether the venue was right for a major conference.

On the other hand, if such a customer visits the hotel to meet you, they may be shown round the hotel and be given coffee or lunch and the best service, but they may not regard this as an infallible sign of how things will be at a later date when they have a group of their company's senior executives with them.

The point is that the salesperson has an important role, not only in selling and doing so persuasively, but in giving a powerful and positive first image of the hotel. The salesperson personifies the hotel and becomes part of the desired test which the customer wants before making a decision; literally, how the sales process is conducted demonstrates service. In practice, of course, these two things have to occur in parallel. So what are the characteristics of what the customer will regard as the 'perfect' hotel/venue salesperson? Some common requirements are as follows.

Appearance

It is common sense to look the part. Standards and practice vary around the world so let me say that, if in doubt, you should remain conventional, smart, professional-looking and remember that seemingly small details matter (for example, clean shoes and fingernails). But do not deceive yourself that a new outfit, or haircut, can replace the need for all the sales technique you can muster. Projecting an appearance of efficiency which is indicative of things is different from being efficient.

For example, your briefcase should be tidy and well-organized, your calculator should have batteries in, visual aids should be ready, accessible, in good condition and in the appropriate order (see Chapter 4). Anything you can think of to enhance this aspect of appearance and build an impression of efficiency is certainly worth a moment's thought. As Oscar Wilde said: 'Only shallow people do not judge by appearances.'

Efficiency

It is not sufficient to *look* efficient, you must *be* efficient. You must:

- be punctual (if you are late what will they anticipate about the timing of coffee breaks in a meeting, or of an early morning wake-up call?);
- remember details and not ask the same question twice (for example, on the telephone at first contact and then when you meet);
- be noticeably prepared;
- clearly be dealing with them on an individual basis, not just going through things so that it seems like a 'standard pitch';
- have all information, facts and figures at your fingertips (and know where to find more, quickly and easily);
- keep promises (as with follow-up action);
- note and use their names;
- be apparently concerned with significant details;
- make notes and be conscious also of the things that allow the customer to be efficient. For example, it may seem very comfortable to sit her on a sofa in the lounge area to discuss

business, but the customer may find sitting in a low chair makes dealing with papers and making notes rather awkward and would prefer to be at a desk or table.

Know your business/'product'

This is vital; and too often inadequate. I once went to a hotel to look at a particular meeting room. The salesperson I saw knew this, yet had none of the facts about it – capacity in terms of accommodating people in different layouts, for example – at their fingertips. Worse, they took ages to find out, and did not seem to have brochures and information that could perhaps have filled the gaps. The net result was that I had little confidence in the place, though it was seemingly ideal in other respects. Think long and hard before you conclude you could never be guilty of this sort of thing; it is all too common.

There are no half-measures in this area. You need to know your venue and its facilities, equipment and services, backwards and inside out. You need to be able to answer any question that potential customers might reasonably put to you and be able to do so promptly, efficiently and without blinding them with technicalities (more of this later). Indeed you will always be vulnerable until you have all the relevant information at your fingertips. You must read brochures, digest the factsheets and manuals. You must walk round and round the place until you know every nook and cranny, and ask questions of others if necessary, until you are satisfied with your knowledge of your venue. When you have done that, keep your knowledge up-to-date. There is no substitute for this, and any shortfall will only dilute the power of your selling; and selling is difficult enough without allowing it to go by default.

Know their business

If knowing *your* business is important, knowing *theirs* is doubly so. Having some basic knowledge about how their business works is important and can be helpful. For example, it will be appreciated if, when you are dealing with an airline, you discuss how you might assist their stopover arrangements in line with their style of customer service. Similarly, a company looking for a venue for a product launch meeting will be reassured if you make it clear you recognize how important it is to their future financial results that it all goes well, that it is not the sort of meeting where it is sufficient for those attending to 'have a nice time'. I once heard a hotel sales executive seeing a client into a meeting at which their company was being put into receivership, say 'Have a good meeting' – hardly an appropriate comment in the circumstances! Beware of such unthinking reflex reactions.

What is most important here is perhaps best described as the area of overlap between their experience and yours. This is best illustrated with a specific example. Consider a discussion with someone wanting to accommodate a meeting, or a training seminar. They do not expect you to understand the content of the training; however, they rightly expect you to understand what goes on in such a meeting and how the various facilities and services of the venue can contribute to its success.

One must grasp the basics of how room layout affects group communication, how important timings are and – some who know me will recognize a hobby-horse here – how an overhead projector is used. Most people who conduct training meetings would no more expect to have a meeting-room without one, than to book into a bedroom and find there was no bed. They are part of the furniture, or should be. They are not, on the other hand, the easiest things to use, and particularly less experienced presenters may find them awkward. Because of this, people want to organize them so that they are set up in the best possible way for them. Their mind will, after all, have other things on it during the meeting. As examples, consider a couple of basic points: some people want space on the same surface the projector is standing on to put slides or lecture notes (the small stands they are sometimes supplied on do not allow this); similarly everyone wants them positioned according to whether they are left- or right-handed as you need to approach them from the correct side. Yet, while I have often been asked whether I want to use an overhead projector, I am very rarely asked anything about how it should be set up and I have never been asked if I am right- or left-handed. Further, I find that two out of three times when I arrive at the venue on the day, the overhead is set up incorrectly

– for example with an acetate roll fixed to run from side to side instead of from the back of the machine forward.

A number of points emerge from this example. First, I hope the importance of an attention to detail is apparent: it matters a great deal. Secondly, it is seen as an indication of the competence of those involved. Customers will feel justified in saying to themselves '. . . if they are in the meetings business and do not even know how an overhead projector works, what else can I have confidence in?' And there is surely no excuse for it. A phrase was used previously to the effect that you are in the business of helping them make their meeting go well, not just providing facilities – and this is the crux of the point.

I believe, you may have gathered, that prevailing standards are poor in this area. Hotels and other venues are full of people selling – pushing is a better word for some – facilities. Yet the reason for highlighting these poor standards is not a critical and negative one – if standards are poor, this represents *a very real opportunity for those who get it right,* because if you do you will surely stand out. You will always do better if you are seen as an expert in whatever the element of the business you are dealing with. Above, we happened to take meetings as an example, but the same principles apply to any aspect of the hotel's service; customers always want matters dealt with in their terms, not yours – and this demands empathy.

Manner
The selling style employed by any salesperson can be character-ized by the interrelation of two factors: projection and empathy. Let us define these terms. *Projection* encompasses everything about the way you come across: power, personality, weight, authority, expertise and what is sometimes called 'clout'. *Empathy* is the ability to put yourself in the other person's place and see things from their point of view. Both are important, but it is the way they are put together that creates an acceptable and appropriate manner; or not. Too much of either holds dangers. Figure 2.1 shows four classic arrangements. This is not intended as an academic view of things, but can provide a way of measuring how you are coming across which can be adjusted as necessary as

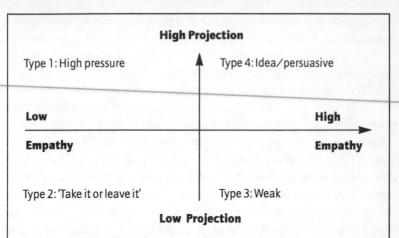

Type 1: the 'high pressure' salesperson is over-aggressive and insensitive. They may feel they win the argument but, in fact, their projection, without empathy, becomes self-defeating and switches people off. The archetypal high-pressure person is the popular image of, say, the insurance salesperson.

Type 2: the 'Take it or leave it' salesperson has little interest in the other person, nor that person's own ideas. A lack of commitment to the whole process tends to let it run into the sand. The archetypal 'Take it or leave it' person is the kind of unhelpful shop assistant with whom most of us are all too familiar.

Type 3: the 'weak' salesperson is one who 'means well'. And so they do. They have good sensitivity to the other person, come across as essentially nice, but take the side of the listener so much that persuasion vanishes and they achieve no commitment.

Type 4: the 'ideal' salesperson is seen as having a creative understanding of the listener, being well-informed and producing both agreement and commitment to the satisfaction of both sides. Being seen to see the other person's point of view is, in itself, crucial.

Figure 2.1: Types of sales approach

you go along. It is possible to categorize four distinct types of sales approach on an axis of high and low projection and high and low empathy. The balance here is important. Both elements contribute to getting the manner right, and either can be overdone. Keeping this balance in mind and actively working to get the right mix will help you be persuasive while being seen by customers as a reasonable person with whom to deal.

Hotels and venues are as respectable an area of selling as any, but in most cultures the salesperson is viewed with at least some suspicion – 'They would say that wouldn't they', being a typical response – so adopting the right manner can improve the way you are seen and the trust and rapport that is built up.

Selling in this area demands that offering advice is part of the sales process, certainly expecting it is part of the buying process. Sometimes this takes the form of an experienced buyer wanting your thoughts on some detail; on other occasions the buyer may be at the opposite extreme and have no experience, they have never organized a wedding before perhaps, and want much detail and advice. You must be able to offer such advice, they must recognize that you can and be prompted to ask, they must trust what they hear and see you as a help and guide to getting what they want, and not simply as a pusher of services.

The right manner is an invaluable aid to selling. It has to be accommodated within your particular style – it is not a matter of typecasting – and the rewards of getting it right benefit both immediate sales success and help cultivate the good long-term arrangements on which your business depends.

Offering hospitality

You are in the hospitality business, so people expect the way you deal with them to reflect your venue's style of service. All the usual courtesies apply: respect for the customer and her views, politeness, concern, willingness to take trouble; all these and more are important. This, to an extent, goes without saying, but hospitality also implies entertaining – and that is worth elaborating on.

Whatever you do must be done well. This applies to the small things, just a cup of tea or coffee, as much as it does to a meal. You need to think about where and how you do the simple things; coffee first and then a look around, or vice versa. On the terrace or in the coffee shop. All the little things count.

Above all, and particularly with longer and more elaborate involvements such as lunch, consider the client and their perception of entertaining. These days most of the people you deal with will be busy. You may have the best restaurant in town, a meal in it may never fail to impress, but not everyone is interested. For some, the last thing they want is another heavy business lunch or the hour and a half it takes up. So never assume the meeting will flow into lunch, and consider alternatives; ask them how long they have, would they prefer a glass of wine and some cheese, and if they opt for a simple and faster alternative, make sure it is planned and delivered well.

One hotel I worked with gave their sales staff a target of so many client lunches per month. I was never very sure about this. It was certainly possible that the person who failed to meet the target was fitting in more meetings than those who did, or that clients were pressed into spending time they did not want and that the exercise ended up leaving the wrong impression as the client hurried back to his office, late for his next meeting. Entertaining is an expensive business too, not so much in terms of the food and drink, but in terms of sales time.

Having dealt with some of the issues in the important matter of manner, we turn to the interrelated area of understanding customers and their circumstances and requirements.

(*Note:* There is a difference between hospitality in the course of the sales process, and bribery. A free weekend for the potential buyer and his wife to help him make up his mind may work well. On the other hand, it may be seen as desperation, or under-handedness, and have the reverse effect. It is also an area that might get you involved in company politics or other hierarchical sensitivities; beware. It is always nice to say 'Thank you' when deserved. A bowl of fruit and note – a personal one rather than the standard printed form – in someone's room or a hundred other gestures can be useful and only take a moment's thought. All this needs to be approached carefully, and there is a cost. One bowl of fruit once is no problem; if a precedent is set and someone then expects one each for the hundreds of people they put up with you, the cost becomes noticeable. Such things also can be regarded by either party as a form of discounting. Nevertheless, the simple things executed with a personal touch can have the greatest impact.)

Understanding customers

Some information about clients comes automatically as part of the interaction with them. They tell you who they are, what they want: a contractual arrangement for 30 bednights per month, a dinner in a private dining-room, a conference for 150 with every sort of projection equipment known to man. But they usually only volunteer so much and are much more likely to tell you *what* they want, than *why*. This area of information represents an important opportunity to make selling somewhat easier and thus make a positive impression on customers and gain an edge on competition. Here we review something of how this can occur.

The wide range of different clients you have to deal with in the hotel business has already been mentioned. All expect you to understand their position and their needs; indeed they will only do business with you, and, if they do, they expect to deal with professionals who are expert in their business. And they define expert as not only understanding your business, but understanding their objectives and requirements. They will be satisfied, and more likely to return, when you not only make the right arrangements for them, but when you help them achieve their objectives. Basic background information is important, but what really achieves differentiation is when you find out the real reasons why they think as they do.

One aspect provides immediate help. Remember that the people you deal with have different reasons for dealing with you and different roles in what is required. For example, with one possible piece of business – a company's annual staff dinner, say – you may deal with a number of people. A secretary charged with all the basic checks of alternative venues (and hoping to avoid the chore of making the actual arrangements); a manager who has been designated to make the arrangement (and is worried that he will never be able to fix something that pleases everyone); and the managing director (who holds the purse strings and sees the whole thing as an unfortunate necessity at a time of other unforeseen expenditure). Clearly the perspective of all these people – and there might be more or their views might be different – are all far apart. All need dealing with in the way best for them, and it is not easy to do so until you know more about their views.

One key principle should be noted here. It is very easy to assume – in what is, after all, the hospitality business – that customer motivation is always positive. This is not the case. Of course, many of the reasons that bring people to hotels are positive: a holiday, a weekend break, a company meeting, all of which may well have social connotations and be designed to be motivational for those attending. On the other hand, many customers, especially business people, are cynical about the whole process; they do not want to stay in another hotel, they have seen it all before and are not easy to impress. Even positive events may conceal difficulties, with something like a wedding involving family feuds and conflicting intentions. I am not suggesting that everything is doom and gloom, but wrong and ill-judged assumptions will not help you to handle things appropriately if they are based on an incorrect premise.

To demonstrate the value and power of true understanding of client needs, we turn now to an example. The following, adapted from a publication I wrote for the Meetings Industry Association, *Comprehending Clients*, takes the form of a typical client situation set out through several sequential stages. It is not intended to catalogue everything that occurs (though reference is made to other stages), but is presented to show how you can make needs come progressively clearer and how this can be used to advantage. It starts with some brief details of the scenario, and this starts with the receipt of an enquiry.

Case Study

The venue

MIA House is located in pleasant countryside, within 100 miles of London. It should be taken as representing a 'country house hotel/management centre' with around a hundred bedrooms and associated meetings space. It is of good quality and caters for a range of clients and uses, from individual business travellers to groups, from meetings to wedding receptions.

The enquiry

This is received in the form of a letter:

WIDGETS INTERNATIONAL LTD
1 June 1995

Dear Sir,

We are planning a meeting in this coming September, which will require a meeting-room and attendant facilities for five days residentially. Delegates will arrive on Sunday evening, business sessions will be conducted throughout the week and during one or two evenings. All meals and breaks will be taken in the chosen venue and a number of specific audio-visual aids will be required. The total number of people involved during the week will be 34.

If this is of interest, and if you feel you can accommodate such an event, perhaps you could telephone me, I can give you any more information you require at that stage and arrange for Mr Graham, our Marketing Manager, and myself to visit you to assess the suitability of your facilities.

Yours sincerely,

Sue Laurie
P.A. to Marketing Manager

With this in mind consider the action and information implications of such an enquiry. The following sets out the kind of approach which is called for:

(i)   Clearly the first place to look is your own organization's files. Have they done business (or made enquiries) in the past?
      If so, what is known about the organization, the people, their requirements? Such a check should include the total venue, not just meetings; do they use the residential side, the restaurants, do they belong to the health club?
(ii) The next step is directories; and there should be a reasonable selection available in the sales office.
      The kind of information which may be useful includes:

- size (numbers of people, offices, amount of turnover);
- activity (product, industry);
- location (nearby, near enough to visit?; far away);
- status (thriving, expanding, in difficulties);
- ownership (are they a subsidiary of something else, or do they have subsidiaries?);
- people (technical, specialist, numerous);

And from these facts, consider the assumptions that can be made: will they be easy or difficult to deal with?; do they represent longer-term potential?; is their area of activity one we know about?; what kind of budget is likely to be involved? Etc.

(iii) What else? Well, if the enquiry warrants it, it may be worth doing a little more checking, for instance:

* Who else may know of them, from a friend of yours to a competitor of theirs?
* Is it worth checking press reports or trade journals?
* Should we get copies of their annual report or sales literature?

Imagine initial checks show the following:

* there has been no prior, recorded contact with this company;
* they are reasonably local, not in the nearest town but within 50 miles;
* they are large (£28m turnover, employing 2,000 people);
* they are manufacturers of Widgets (and unspecified industrial components like, say, ball-bearings or gearwheels), a leader in their field, internationally recognized as a quality supplier and apparently expanding;
* it is a company with no subsidiaries, though they have offices in several main centres around the country.

With this information in mind, a phone call can be made to set a date for a visit. Remember, the letter asked for such a call. If it had not been so specific, then there are other options. A letter, and brochures, could have been sent first, followed by a telephone call. The scenario we are following describes one, albeit typical, situation. Remember also that a meeting seems highly probable, there may be a case for making a brief telephone call, with the key objective of setting up the date. Alternatively, it might be useful to discover more about the planned event, asking questions to obtain this information first, to check that we can accommodate it suitably; secondly, to give ourselves more information to act as a basis to the next meeting.

What is done will depend on the feeling we receive from the client. Are they happy to answer questions? Or will they see it as being like the Spanish Inquisition, at a stage when they have not even seen the venue? We will assume, for the sake of the continuing scenario, that we judge that some questions will be seen as acceptable. There are, of course, a host of details which must ultimately be obtained, ranging from more exact timings and audio-visual requirements, to whether they want 'No smoking' signs or ashtrays.

Many of these are details, and while all are important, can wait until a later stage. What is important at this stage is information which will help the meeting with Widgets International go well. Someone has to decide:

* what they are likely to want to see;
* who they should meet;

- where discussions should be held;
- what preparation and briefing of other members of staff is necessary.

All this, and more, must be planned so as to ensure that the encounter is persuasive. So, questioning at this stage must focus on any details which are key, e.g.: the exact date; more exact bedroom requirements; are single/twin or double rooms required?; what meeting accommodation is required?; rather than the more detailed facilities required, which can be more conveniently checked at a later time.

We will leave the techniques of exactly how you ask questions in a way that will be acceptable to the client and obtain the information you want precisely, quickly and easily on one side for the moment. This is picked up, in context of the overall sequence of sales techniques, in Chapter 6.

In addition, other areas are typically investigated in similar situations, e.g.:

Topic	*Questions*
Nature of the meeting.	'What kind of meeting is it?'
Who is involved in the meeting/venue decision?	'Are you making all the arrangements?' 'Will you be there during the function?'
Other facilities.	'Are any leisure facilities important?'

Apart from the danger of being seen to be getting into too much detail at this stage – after all, they may feel they want to see that the venue is suitable before going much further – any information is, directly or potentially, useful.

What do we now know? Assuming answers to the points raised above, a meeting might start with the following facts now known, in addition to what is stated in their letter, and what was discovered from research.

Reply from Widgets International
When Sue was spoken to on the telephone, she added the following:

- '... no exact date has been fixed, but the latter part of the month is likely to be better.'
- 'Yes, everyone will be arriving on Sunday, though not all at the same time.'
- 'Everyone will need to be accommodated in single rooms.'
- 'Four break-out rooms will be required, with working groups of 7/8 in each.'
- 'It's a product briefing session.'
- 'Yes, though Mr Graham will decide which venue is suitable – and we will both attend throughout.'
- 'I am not sure about leisure facilities, I will mention that to Mr Graham and we can plan to be more specific when we meet.'

For the sake of the example we will continue to assume here that the requirement is reasonably clear, and the information reasonably forthcoming.

Additional information

During such a telephone conversation and at subsequent meetings, this level of information must be filled out somewhat. Remember, the customer's prime concern is not organizing meeting space and facilities, it is making sure their meeting goes well, that it achieves its objectives. It is not the existence of facilities, or even the excellence of them, that will prompt them to make a firm arrangement with a supplier; but their perception of the likelihood of achieving this at a particular venue.

Further, unless they have used the facilities before (and remember Widgets International have not) they cannot test how well their meeting will work. They will judge the likelihood from what they see, and how they are dealt with. And, as has been said, they will look for clear signs of an understanding of them, and their particular requirements, as part of this judgement. This makes it very important to know not only *what* they want, but *why* they want it – and to understand the circumstances from their point of view.

Consider for a moment: what do they mean when they say 'It is a product briefing session'? It is not, in fact, very clear. It is what might be called background information. If we are to be seen as better informed than our competitors, then we must get beyond this level of information. This has implications for the questioning techniques used, a point we pick up later. Returning now to the example question which started this review of 'additional information' – 'What kind of meeting is it?' and the answers suggested, consider what is now known:

- it is a product briefing;
- it is an unusual and important gathering;
- the people attending are senior, important and from all over the world;
- the financial outcome is potentially high;
- confidential matters will be discussed.

In addition, we might realistically infer (or, ask more questions to verify) that:

- timing will be important;
- participants may have complex travel arrangements, and arrive first at the airport;
- different diets may need catering for;
- language could be a problem;
- the social element, amongst senior people gathering infrequently, will be important;
- the total cost of the whole (product launch) will be considerable;
- it is a busy time in the company.

There may be signs of more than this and, overall, it is reasonable to assume they will only book a venue in which they have considerable confidence, in the sense that it will fit with these points and more.

Further, in terms of using this information, the line of discussion has made it clear that we do understand, and we are now able to refer back to their statements so that we can say later: 'Because of the confidential nature of the meeting you indicated, if we locate it' rather than saying: 'I expect the meeting is confidential, therefore I suggest ' (you may be wrong), or not picking up the point at all; all of which helps position us as the caring expert, sensitive to exactly what is necessary to help their meeting go well. So, in this way, via whatever contacts are going on, the information about client needs can become clearer, and do so in a straightforward manner which is acceptable and apparent to the client. Certainly we are becoming much better informed about Widgets International. But there is another dimension we must take into account, and if we obtain good information in this area also our position will be stronger still. This concerns the people involved.

Read the background information about the three main people involved in Widget's September meeting: John Graham, the Marketing Manager; Sue Laurie, his personal assistant; and David Kirby, the Product Manager (whose product is the subject of the product briefing of the meeting). Ask yourself two questions:

(i) Of this information, what would it be reasonable and possible to discover?
(ii) How would these points be specifically helpful in selling, or servicing the event?

John Graham

John is a fairly typical marketing manager. Now 45, he began his career with an engineering degree, worked as a sales engineer, and moved up the sales side of another components firm. As an area manager, he has spent two years in the Far East on a project setting up distribution in Asia-Pacific, and returned to the UK where he had an offer to become Sales Manager for Widgets International. He did well in his position and, as the company expanded, became their first Marketing Manager in 1990. If all continues well he should be a Board Director within a year. He is well paid for what he does, both in salary and with a profit-sharing scheme; he is married with two boys and lives in a small village some fifteen miles from the town where Widgets is located.

John's responsibilities are world-wide. However, he has a good team and is himself a good manager, prepared to delegate and use key people around him. Those who are immediately important to him in this respect are the two product managers, comparatively new members of the team, made necessary by the expansion of sales and product lines, the sales manager and, of course, his personal assistant.

He is currently concerned that, after a slight spell of 'marking time' in the recent period of economic uncertainty, the company now moves ahead. This is dependent in large part on the success of the new product (the Superwidget), which is being launched first in key overseas markets which have been so important to the company's development (and assisted spreading the risk during the recent economic difficulties in the UK). He plans to work closely with David Kirby, who has not been involved in such a project before, to ensure the success of the launch.

The planned meeting is an important part of the launch, he will keep an eye on the arrangements, but is happy to leave the details to Sue Laurie. His visit with her to MIA House is as much to brief her on the requirements for the event, as to vet the venue itself. The budget responsibility is, of course, his and not unimportant – but so is the success of the event. He will, in fact, be overseas for part of July and August (he travels a good deal), as well as having some holiday planned during the school holidays.

Sue Laurie

Sue is 26, a competent secretary, now in a position where she is a 'genuine PA' able to develop the executive part of her job and feel she is making a real contribution. She joined Widgets three years ago from a smaller firm, and worked first in the Customer Service department as secretary not only to the sales office manager, but handling work for others in the department, and also taking her share of some of the ongoing contact with customers. Coming from marketing and at a stage when she wanted more responsibility, she kept her eyes and ears open for other opportunities and applied at once when John Graham's previous secretary left to get married and moved away. She has worked for him for almost a year. The relationship works well and both feel she is very much part of the team. She is progressively becoming more involved in the activities, and is pleased that he allows time to brief her and encourage such involvement. His absences from the office make it necessary that he can rely on things being well-managed in his absence; the amount he has to do means he will leave things to her where he can – whether he is at Head Office or not.

She sees the job as a possible first step out of the secretarial area, and works hard to make it work. A good organizer, she has been with the company sufficiently long to know the people, how things work and deal with an increasing number of matters on her own.

While she has not previously organized the kind of event contemplated, she feels well able to do so, and already knows a good deal about the circumstances of the meeting and its importance. Perhaps she underestimates, at this stage, some of the detail involved, but she knows she will attend throughout and is looking forward to meeting a number of the participants with whom she has had long-distance communication. Her one worry is being able to play her part in the event and keep things from becoming disrupted by her absence, along with a number of others, from the office during the period of the meeting. Not so cynical as her travel-weary boss, she is also looking forward to staying in what she assumes will be an attractive hotel, and as a keen exerciser and swimmer hopes it will have good leisure facilities to make up for the expected larger-than-usual food intake.

David Kirby

David is a 28-year-old business graduate. He took an MBA at Cranfield Management College, and, while no academic genius, did well at it. He regards himself as a professional, though in reality his experience is limited. At the time he started work, the MBA did not prove quite the passport to instant success he had hoped. He joined a large firm in a rather old-fashioned industry, and progress was not only slow, but likely to remain so as most key managers, a management team who were older than average, seemed keen to hang onto things and protect the *status quo.*

Despite this he gained some good practical experience, enough to look round for a better opportunity, in a company prepared to give him more responsibility and greater involvement internationally. Widgets International, advertising a new position clearly linked to expansion, seemed to fit the bill. He got on well with John Graham, who he felt was prepared to give the successful candidate a real chance to make something of the job. While little was said of the launch of Superwidgets when he joined the company some nine months ago, it was now clear that its launch would have a major effect on his position and career, as it was a key part of the company's development for the future. He was well able to cope with the process. In many ways it played to his strengths. The plans, the budgets, the strategy – the whole process had gone well. Starting the launch process overseas had been his idea, and now approved, made a sound basis for proceeding further – provided the meeting went well and the necessary support and commitment was gained.

If David had weaknesses they lay in a combination of comparative inexperience and in his communication skills. He had never seen formal presentation as one of his strengths, and as the importance of the event and the major role he would have to play in it became clearer to him, this aspect did worry him. At least he was sufficiently bright to be aware of this, and he realized also that he had a good deal to learn about the nature and motivations of those attending. There was much preparation to be done, a deadline that appeared increasingly tight, and his secretary (Gill Nathan, whom he shares with his fellow product manager), is already feeling the load.

Much of the information given about the three individuals would specifically not be discovered, certainly not early on, and would be of little use in any case. On the other hand, the background and more personal details may be useful as a relationship develops over time. Certainly it shows how such factors affect the way people are likely to operate. So, here we concentrate on more immediate factors:

John Graham

Information (you might discover)	*How it might help*
He is a senior member of the company, has responsibility for the event and is the ultimate decision-maker.	We know where power lies, and can deal with it accordingly.

He has an experience of the international side, and responsibility for the new product launch.	He is likely to know what he wants.
He rates the project highly, and needs it to go well.	This is likely to affect his view of many of the details of the event.
At the meeting it is likely to be clear that he will leave much of the detail to his PA.	This will help subsequent contact.
He will be away for some of the run-up time.	We will need to know the deadlines and lines of authorities.

Sue Laurie

Information (you might discover)	*How it might help*
She is a competent 'real' PA to whom much is delegated.	She will be key to the decision and organization.
She will be 'in charge' when her boss is away.	We must have her 'on our side'.
She has not previously been through this process of organization (though it is likely to be clear that she knows the importance of the event and how its success can reflect on her).	We can position ourselves as 'adviser' – who can ensure all goes well.
Her lack of experience may affect details.	We must help her 'think of everything'.
She is concerned about communications between the venue and the office during the event.	This must be set up efficiently.
She is personally looking forward to the experience of a nice hotel.	We may be able to 'spoil' her.

David Kirby

Note: He will not be at the first meeting, and where people other than those you have met are clearly important to the situation, it is worth making an effort to find out something about them. Certainly here, if we can discover it, there is useful information.

Information (you might discover)	*How it might help*
He is new to the company. As this is a major event, he is likely to be particularly concerned that it goes well. It is his idea; another reason why it must go well.	He will relate best to those who give the greatest certainty of this (and seek this reassurance from Sue and John).
His presentation weakness is key. He may be worried, concerned about details, perhaps even looking for reassurance.	If we can help – by attention to details and precise arrangements – to make it easier, he will see us as an asset.
He may well be being told to leave the detail to Sue, but will no doubt be concerned to brief her.	If we can suggest a meeting, direct contact may help.

Note: Again there are no 'right' answers, you may feel other points are also important. What is clear from this sort of analysis is that the three people will have different views and priorities regarding the event and must be dealt with in different ways as a result. Certainly the information possibilities are made clear by such a picture, whichever elements may be discovered at whatever stage.

Our example seems to indicate reasonably straightforward clients. But clients are not always either reasonable or straight-forward, and even the best of them 'have their moments', so it is worth bearing in mind other aspects of what may be in the clients' minds. Earlier in this chapter it was suggested that negative views might be important here; prompted by the case and continuing to bear in mind a meeting requirement, we consider some specifics. Customers may be:

- unclear on requirements;
- changing their minds (constantly);
- undecided on dates;
- unreasonably demanding, about standards and service;
- nit-picking with regard to detail;
- uncontactable at key times;
- simply disorganized;
- difficult about reasonable, or even standard, contract terms and fussy, officious, condescending, abrupt and stubborn.

Any of this can make them difficult to deal with; a number of these characteristics occurring together, and smooth client relations may seem an impossible dream. There is no doubt that, on occasions, an old adage of the meetings industry along the lines of 'It would all be so much easier if it wasn't for the client' holds some truth.

However, as the saying has it: '*No* customer is worse than no *customer*'. Clients are – well – clients and if we can cope with even their most difficult moments, we do better at finding them and developing their business. Maybe it will be just a little easier if we understand their 'twitches'; why are they like this?

The first part of the answer concerns a number of fundamental truths which we must accept and work with, rather than fight against. For example:

- For most clients, doing business with meetings industry suppliers is not their major concern. They are busy running their lives and businesses; sometimes their contacts with us are seen as an annoying, peripheral, time-wasting chore – the reverse, of course, of how we see it.
- For many, hotels and venues are far from glamorous. They talk about 'another night away' – 'too many hotel lunches' and would actually rather be at home (or in the office) getting on with their lives.
- For many, meetings involve travel and more often this is at best a chore, at worst an uncomfortable nightmare. No one looks forward to hours driving on a busy motorway in pouring rain, however attractive the destination.

These, and other factors, may sometimes be difficult to accept if we proceed only on the basis of our involvement in, and enjoyment of, the meetings business.

In addition, many meetings situations present real problems to those on the client side. They worry – and we do not, as a result, always see them at their best. For example, remember:

- How much may be hanging on a meeting – money, reputations, position, career, publicity – all may be affected in the few hours or days a meeting takes up; and sometimes affected dramatically.
- People may be in unfamiliar territory, doing things they find new, difficult or awkward. This may range from simple organizational factors (selecting menus their colleagues will approve) to a regularly more significant one, that of presentation. Most meetings involve it to some degree or another; even experienced speakers may be nervous, some will be petrified (in surveys public speaking is always in the top two or three 'worst fears'); all will be concerned to see it goes well.
- Deadlines may be difficult for you, but they are for clients as well; time pressure will always tend to increase stress.
- Equipment involved – unfamiliar equipment – increases the fear of something going wrong ('Will they be able to see the slides – will they be right way up?').

Such fears are understandable, or should be; but they may be compounded by the meetings industry if care is not taken at every stage:

- Are clients clear who they should deal with about what?
- Can they find who they need, fast?
- Is the documentation clear?
- Are they sure they understand, particularly what for them are technical details?

Too often clients report that meetings-industry people, by being insensitive or fighting against these factors, can end up making matters worse – something that is unlikely to reinforce any good opinion they may have formed of you.

There is one simple rule to remember: everything you do must make it easier for them to achieve their objectives. Clients buy from, and deal with, people who understand and assist them in resolving their problems.

Here are some examples of what we can do.

For the nervous presenter:
- make sure the speaking area is comfortable for them;
- demonstrate (carefully) how equipment works;
- suggest, encourage rehearsal;
- let them try out, and see, how slides appear;
- demonstrate the acoustics or microphone, and watch for any details (e.g. a left-handed person will need an overhead projector in a different position from a right-handed one).

For the organizer:
- make sure they have seen and are happy with all the facilities they may need;
- give them a note of the names (and extension numbers) of the key people they may need to contact 'on the day';
- confirm all details they would see as necessary in writing;
- ensure you issue a clear map of your location.

If you can become sensitive to such issues you will improve the way you relate to clients, and the image they form of you and your organization. There are issues here we will pick up in reviewing what actually should go on in a sales meeting; for the moment the question of the clients' position in the overall process should be clear. It is vital that consideration of this pervades everything done in selling.

Everything covered in this chapter helps provide a basis for what you do in selling. Remember, selling is helping people to buy, and so must be based on the customer, their needs, their situation and perspective. Tackled on this basis you have a much better chance of making a powerful impression on your clients, and they will have a positive impression of you which will help secure the relationship. Before we can deploy this sort of thinking through, or consider the sales technique that goes with it, there has to be someone to sell to; sales success depends on having a constant supply of new contacts to talk to (as well as maintaining contact with past users and contacts), and it is to this topic that we turn in the next chapter.

3 New blood: prospecting and making an initial approach

W HAT IS REQUIRED to fill a venue, and if possible to fill it to a consistent level in all departments, is a mixture of repeat and new business. If no one ever came back, sales would have an impossible task – and service standards would need a major overhaul! Customer management and the job of ensuring that contact is maintained in a way that encourages people to come back for more, and develops their business so that it is worth more, is the subject of Chapter 7. Here we look first at how you can identify new prospects and then at how you can make effective initial contact with them. Some new business comes in prompted in ways other than by individual sales action. For instance, some enquiries will come from promotional activity, in direct relationship to how persuasive such activity is. Here we are concerned with what has to be initiated additionally by the salespeople. Who to contact is dependent on who is most likely to be a real prospect for a particular property, and this in turn is dependent on some analysis. A number of questions should be considered.

Why should customers do business with you?

Consider 'product advantage'. Do you offer particular benefits in terms of: size, location, price, 'style', service or combinations of these and other factors? And how do you compare with your immediate (and less direct) competitors? Perhaps your car park capacity matches your conference room capacity when others fall short; your air-conditioning is quiet when others are not; you have a swimming pool and others do not; your bar is more friendly and pub-like than another (or has better – less expensive – prices).

What kind of customer is most likely to do business with you?

This needs to be considered in the light of the above; and it is important because so very many people are in fact some sort of prospect, but time and resources of course prohibit contacting every potential user, particularly the smaller or less likely prospects. Answering this question focuses prospecting activity on a manageable number of priority prospects and will help improve sales productivity. Ask yourself if the best prospects are likely to be:

- local, or within a specific radius (again productivity affects this);
- individuals or organizations.

In the case of organizations, are the best prospects:

- large (in the number of people employed);
- in any particular industry;
- those who have a good growth record, high staff turnover, or exhibit the greatest growth and development?

Also, ask who within the organization is the best contact (it may well be more than one person in a large organization): a director, manager or secretary; in which functional area: marketing, production, computers, training or personnel? All this then brings us to the next question.

What do we need to know about them?

Certainly before you set out to contact anyone individually, you need to know a little about them. Some research may be worthwhile. You will definitely need to know what business they are in, and you may need to know more about the business: what size it is; the number of people it employs; how the business is going; and whether they obviously have need for your kind of services. (For example, a company in a fast-changing field such as, say information technology, which also employs a large number of people, may well undertake a good deal of training and therefore have a regular requirement for external meeting rooms. Similarly, an international firm may have a regular need to accommodate visitors from overseas.)

With the picture of the 'ideal prospect' this thinking helps clarify in your mind, you can then turn to actually identifying the names of individual organizations and people to contact.

Prospecting 'systems'

The first rule to get the most from prospecting is absurdly simple: you must do it. Somehow, perhaps because it is inevitably less attractive (and more difficult) than contacting the people you know already, many salespeople do less of it than they intend; other things seem to take up too much time, something that is inclined to be especially true in the hotel business where operational matters can sometimes also intrude.

Prospecting is, as much as anything, a state of mind. Of course there are techniques, prompts and systems that help make it happen, but much of the onus is on the individual, and those who cultivate the habit of regular prospecting tend to produce more in sales than those who rely only on their existing customers and contacts.

The first step is to ensure that some ongoing processes are in place to help ensure that prospecting becomes an automatic part of the daily pattern of activity. If this can be done, coupled with a good strike rate once steps are taken to make contact, then more will be achieved, and this will show in the sales figures. The following list is illustrative of the principles of regular prospecting methodology.

Endless chain

This is simply using one prospect to lead to another. A first may come, let us say, as an enquiry. Once you know who they are, what they might be interested in, why they came to you, then you can ask who else they can direct you to. This may be by asking: 'Do you know anyone else who might be interested?', and analysis: 'If this bank manager is interested, which others can I talk to?'

Centres of influence

These are people or organizations through whom you may make contact with numbers of prospects on a regular basis, because they have the power to introduce or recommend. They may include trade and professional bodies, chambers of commerce, associations, banks and others. It is worth thinking through which may be useful in your business, listing them and systematically keeping in touch to ensure they know of you, know something about what you do, and are reminded of this and kept up-to-date. (Share the task of keeping in touch with colleagues, each taking responsibility for a number of such contacts.) Any contact which can lead to numbers of new customers is likely to be both worthwhile and cost-effective if contact is maintained systematically.

Personal observation

If you develop the habit of being observant, then a regular supply of new prospects can follow. First, consider things in print. You need to review regularly any journals, newspapers or pub-lications of relevance to your business sectors. Trade or industry journals are a good example. So are in-house newsletters if you have major companies as customers who produce them and, yes, they will often put you on the list – provided you ask. News of companies, developments, staff changes, re-locations and more can all provide information to lead you to a new prospect.

Secondly, keep your eyes open and check anything that might help you. Ask yourself: who has moved into the new office block on the corner or into the office next door to someone you have already visited? Such observation, and perhaps a little associated research, can lead to new names and thus new prospects.

Chance contacts

This is closely related to personal observation, but worth a separate mention. The author has twice obtained work following a conversation with someone sitting next to him on an aeroplane, when idle chatter identified common business interests. And once he even got work from someone whose office he wandered into, lost, to seek directions in the bowels of an office block. Beware, of course, of taking this too far, but keep an eye open for such opportunities, particularly in places where people of similar interests meet – a trade association meeting, perhaps.

'Cold canvass'

Simply knocking on doors is probably not to be recommended to anyone but the least faint-hearted. However, one variant may well be useful. In places where different businesses exist close by each other, such as on an industrial estate or in an office block, it may be worth knocking on some doors near to an existing visit; not to try to sell them something, but to discover names. Ask the receptionist who is in charge of hotels and travel arrangements or whatever. Again, even a few new names may be useful and they will be geographically convenient too – which aids your productivity if you subsequently need to visit them regularly.

List

Not so much the big ones like *Yellow Pages*, but the small specialist, or local ones. Association membership lists, interest groups, sports clubs; whatever ties in with your business areas. This can yield names for small mailings, and can be made manageable by being reviewed progressively with mailshots then sent at so many per week (remembering that even quite small numbers sent on a regular basis can provide powerful promotion over the year). Some research on what lists exist is often well worthwhile.

Past clients/contracts

If you are systematic there should be few of these; but there will be some. People have good reasons sometimes for stopping doing business with you – someone leaves the company, a budget is cut, expenditure is delayed, or actively changed. This being so, always check when things may change again, note it in the diary, however far ahead, and remember to get in touch again and keep in touch as appropriate during any enforced gap. Of course, if you have not been very systematic in the past, it may well be worth doing a comprehensive research of the 'archives'. Remember, a customer for one aspect of your range of services, but not for another, may be persuaded to buy both. One hotel discovered it could boost its restaurant trade by mailing its business meetings clients, who were recorded in a separate file and previously neglected.

Suppliers

Anyone you do business with might be persuaded to do business with you if your service is something they buy. You know them; they know you. They doubtless want to retain your business, so they are unlikely to reject out of hand a suggestion to talk. You will no doubt have a good record of such people in your accounts department – everything from office equipment suppliers to laundries – and need to do little more than check through the invoices they send you to identify them and compile a contact list.

Extra-curricular activities

Business and pleasure do not always mix, but sometimes they do. A good number of business deals really are struck on the golf course just as legend would have it. It may be worth reviewing what you do, where you go, what clubs or associations you belong to, and seeing whether you can get more from them in a business sense. This is worth a thought but definitely needs to be the subject of care; after all, the committee may not approve of overt canvassing (though if you were on the committee maybe you would make more contacts).

Directories

There are so many directories published that, certainly in the UK, there is an annual directory of directories published. This implies there could well be one or more that could be useful to you, that you do not currently know about. Check it out, even one with just a few new names can be useful.

Once methods such as those above have produced the names of potentially good prospects then you need to make contact. There are essentially two options: write to them; or telephone them, or you can use a combination of the two, sending a letter first, for instance, and then following up on the telephone once this has been received (a combination that often works well).

Making contact

Let us assume you telephone and letters are sent later. The first thing to do is think about what your objective is in calling them – it is to sell them the hotel. But is it? Is this reasonable? How many people book a dinner and dance, or anything else for that matter, on hearing you, and perhaps hearing of your property, for this first time on the telephone? Very few. So what are your objectives: to obtain information (who is the decision-maker?) or to make an appointment? If the latter, when and where will that be? Ideally you want them to come and see the property, but not everyone will make that amount of time and effort at an early stage. It can mean giving up an hour or two, more perhaps if travel time is longer. Many more clients in recent days are resistant to this; their time is valuable and they may agree to your going to see them initially in order to form a first judgement of whether a visit is worthwhile. This may reduce your productivity somewhat, indeed it may be a more difficult meeting away from the hotel, but if you ignore this requirement then you may well miss some good prospects.

Assuming you are aiming for a meeting, the next question to consider is when you ideally want to see them. What is best here will depend on where the meeting is to be; if they are visiting you there may be times when activities at the hotel make it more or less suitable – you do not want someone arriving to discuss quiet weekend breaks at the same time as a large party of Japanese tourists arrives at Reception. Equally, there may be impressive things going on that make for a more impressive 'show-round'. There are the logistics and the conveniences to you to consider; you do not just want to see them 'as soon as possible', but at a time and date that suits your schedule and productivity. Beware of suspect 'stated wisdom', such as 'No buyer wants to see you before 10 a.m.', when in fact some will not only happily see you at 8.30 a.m. but you are unlikely to have an uninterrupted hour until the switchboard opens. Neither should you believe that 'No buyer will see you after 4 p.m. or on Fridays'.

In fact, everyone's habits are different, and you simply risk restricting your opportunities if you make unwarranted assumptions.

With the answers to all the foregoing in mind it is now time to think about actually making an appointment. Ultimately, even if a letter has been sent, you will soon find yourself on the telephone. The telephone is a form of communication that presents both problems and opportunities. It is not everyone's favourite kind of call, but a structured approach helps. You still will not win them all, but you will get a better success rate; and if you do that, at every stage, you will sell more in the end. Before we speak to the prospect, however, there is still something else to consider.

Getting through to the right person

This is not just a matter of defeating the mechanical gremlins of the telephone company, but being able to make direct contact with the decision-maker. This difficulty alone can get salespeople off to an uneasy start in prospecting. Switchboards and secretaries are often masters at spotting, and refusing, anyone who is selling.

Some simple rules will help you overcome this problem.

In 'cold calling', prior research may have given you the name you want. If not, always ask for the name first and then ask to be put through. Then ask to speak to him. You may be put straight through and you will know as he answers 'Morris here' that you have the right person, avoiding the need to check who he is as he answers. Operators and secretaries will often put a call through to a department or assistant first rather than the manager himself. Alternatively, more questioning may follow:

Operator: Who is calling Mr Morris?

Salesman: Mr Roberts (note: though saying 'Roberts. John Roberts' takes a moment longer and, as switchboard operators are busy, reduces the time for further inquiry. It also somehow sounds more as if you know who you are asking for.)

At this stage, you may be put through, particularly if you say your name confidently. The same applies to the question 'What company are you with?' You should answer confidently and without volunteering any extra information. The really protective switchboard operator will then ask 'What are you calling about?' Avoid clichés and dishonest answers, e.g. 'a research survey', and describe briefly and comprehensively what you want to discuss (not what you want to sell), e.g. 'I need to talk to Mr Morris about the time and cost of setting up your training events'. A secretary/operator is unlikely to want to get involved in the detail of what may by then sound a little complicated and you should, at this point, get through.

For regular or follow-up contacts the same principles apply, at least if there remains a chance your prospect would rather not speak to you. It is useful to refer back to past events, e.g. 'I agreed with Mr Morris when I saw him last month that I would call this week'. Only phrase it this way if it was agreed; alternatively say 'I said to Mr Morris . . .' or, having written suggesting you call him on a particular day, 'Mr Morris is expecting to hear from me today'. (This kind of approach can also be used as a follow-up to the right kind of phrase in a selling/prospecting letter.) If the buyer is not at the office, the secretary may offer to help or take a message. The most useful piece of information you can obtain is when the contact will be available to take a call. Ask 'May I call back this afternoon?' or 'Will he be available tomorrow morning?' This saves you time in further wasted calls and means that you can tell the operator next time, 'I arranged with Mr Morris's secretary to call him at about this time'. If all else fails, and a secretary is totally intransigent, then one trick that sometimes works is to telephone at lunchtime. Try at 12.30 p.m. say, and if she is there then try again at 1.30 p.m. and you may well get through directly to the contact you want; most people are not 'guarded' every moment of the day.

Whatever kind of call you are making, it is necessary to get through to the right person; what follows depends on the nature of the call and your objectives.

Making the appointment

Whoever you are calling, whether it is someone who has seen a brochure, responding to an advertisement or mailshot, or simply a 'cold prospect', think about the call before you make it. Before you even dial the prospect's number, you must have at hand the following:

- all customer information available, including any 'Personal hints', which can help avoid simple gaffes such as the wrong pronunciation of someone's name;
- information on your availability for appointments;
- a checklist of the information you ideally want – other services being used by the customer, their preferences, size of company, or whatever is relevant.

Once you are through to the right person – and this is worth checking, particularly if you have been transferred more than once – you need a structured approach to give you the best chance of success. There are seven key stages to follow (some taking only a few seconds) when making the majority of such calls.

1. A greeting

Greetings should be kept short, simple and to the point. It may be no more than 'Good morning', and can link to a check that you have a successful connection, 'Is that John Robertson?'

2. Identification

Any identification should be clear and, allowing how bad many people are at retaining a name, may contain an element of repetition, 'My name is Forsyth, Patrick Forsyth, from Touchstone Training & Consultancy'. Then, allowing for any response, move promptly into the next stage.

3. Reason for calling

Your reason that you give for calling must be customer-orientated, containing a benefit, and explaining why you want an appointment (do not try to sell the whole property and all its services at this stage), perhaps mentioning something the customer will be able to see, touch, try out or have demonstrated at the meeting, something which can only take place at a meeting.

It helps to speak of the meeting as 'working with the customer' (rather than 'doing something to them'), for instance 'When we meet we can go through the details together and make sure we come to the right solution'. This creates a feeling of customer orientation. One thing is vitally important here, doubly so as it is often not well done, and that is to get a good descriptive way of saying something succinct about your property. So many salespeople start with: 'It is a medium-sized hotel, with 127 rooms and two restaurants, as well as a full range of function rooms . . .' Not surprisingly people at the other end are not usually on the edges of their seats about this ('Two restaurants! Wow, tell me more . . .') – it needs thinking about and may be worth practising: something that you can do, in private if you wish, with a small cassette recorder. Alternatively try it out on a colleague. It is very easy to find what you habitually say has become somewhat mundane.

4. Request for appointment

There is no substitute for asking for an appointment. However, bear in mind the following:

- Mention the duration of the meeting. Honestly. It is no good pretending you only need 30 minutes if you need an hour. At worst you may arrive and find they have only exactly the 30 minutes you asked for on the telephone.
- Give the customer a reasonable lead time. Many are less likely to refuse an appointment for seven to ten days' time than to refuse an appointment for tomorrow.
- Offer an alternative. 'Would 3 p.m. Thursday afternoon be suitable, or would you prefer a morning, say Wednesday morning?' State the first option more precisely than the second.

5. Respond to objections

Now and again resistance will be met, but you can then employ an objection-handling technique called the 'boomerang' technique. This is particularly useful for 'turning' an objection to your advantage. For instance:

Prospect: 'It's not convenient – I haven't the time.'

Salesperson: 'It's because I know you're busy that a short meeting may be useful. It will give you the opportunity to hear how we go about things and see whether scheduling more time for discussion or a visit is worthwhile.'

When you have got them back on track again, and sounding even tentatively agreeable, you can 'close' again as fast as is polite – with the appointment as your objective. If it is impossible to make an appointment, you can still get something from the situation by getting some new information for the records. Having 'won' the conversation and 'negotiation' to that point, the prospect will often be in the frame of mind to allow you some concessions, and may be quite willing to give you information about future plans, changes or the names of others in the organization you could contact, etc.

Further examples of objection handling can be seen, if we look at the four different types of objections you may encounter.

The unspoken objection

This is difficult to overcome. It is there, real enough, in the prospect's mind, but is unspoken. Without any feedback other than voice (a puzzled look is not visible over the telephone), you must literally 'read between the lines' to discover when this is happening. If you believe it is, then you should ask questions and encourage the prospect to raise whatever is on their mind. This works even to the point of suggesting hesitation: 'I detect a slight hesitation, are you sure Friday is OK? I could equally well do one day next week'; or 'You sound unsure, I do want to make sure the time is convenient for you; does it really suit?'

The legitimate objection

This is a genuine reason for a prospect's lack of interest. But it may be short-lived, the need may arise later or someone else in the organization might respond positively. If so, the following approaches would be relevant:

Prospect	Salesperson
'I'm right in the middle of the budget preparation: I can't see anyone right now.'	'I understand, Mrs Smith. When would be a better time for me to call you back?'
'Thanks for calling, but that kind of decision is outside my authority. It would be a waste of time for us to meet.'	'OK, thanks for that, Mr Black. May I ask who I should contact. Can I say you referred me to them?'
'Look, before you go any further, I can't see us needing your services. We booked something similar a few months ago and, unless there's a remarkable growth in the market we're fully set up for the foreseeable future.'	'Ah, I see. Then clearly a meeting now would seem unproductive. I wonder if, rather than us meeting now, you could give me some background information over the phone . . . Thank you very much, Mr Cooper. I'd like to call you again in three months when the growth you spoke about may well have happened.'

One other form of legitimate objection is a complaint about a minor, but real, disadvantage; a perceived, but incorrect, product limitation; or a negative past relationship. In all these cases the response should be the same:

- *accept* the prospect's point of view without necessarily agreeing with it;
- *minimize* or correct the point of view by repeating the objection in your own words in the form of a question, and playing down its real or perceived impact;
- *compensate* by referring to one or more definite advantages which outweigh the small disadvantage.

The false objection

A false objection is the prospect's argument or excuse for not granting an appointment for a face-to-face interview or visit. As the name implies, it is not the real reason for avoiding a meeting. For example:

'Your venue just isn't the sort of place we use.'	He or she is hiding a true objection: what is it that makes the target say this?
'I'm not interested.'	He or she needs more information to become interested.
'Your prices are too high.'	The real meaning here is that the desire for the product is too low.

To overcome these objections you must ask questions and get the prospect to reveal his or her true objection to meeting with you. For example, if the point is made that prices are too high, you might say, 'Of course, it is a substantial amount of money, but when you say that, what are you comparing it with?'; this is to focus the conversation on the real feelings.

'Classic' telephone objections

Prospects frequently state an objection rather than put the phone down on a sales caller. Such objections sometimes have a grain of truth in them but often they are used as part of a game that prospects play to test your resolve and persistence, or your professionalism (are you reading a telescript?) or give the impression that they are less available for an interview than may actually be the case. The tone of their voice, persistence of objection or conviction in their own objection will give you an indication of whether an objection is of this nature. The quicker a prospect positively responds to and accepts your reply to an objection, the more likely it is that it will have been this sort. For example:

Prospect	**Salesperson**
'You're just trying to sell me something.'	'No. It's too early to say that! First we must explore your needs and see what sort of benefits you consider important.'
'You'll be wasting your time giving me a sales pitch.'	'That's one thing I won't do. What I would like to do is discuss how we can help. I'm sure our time wouldn't be wasted.'
'Look, just give me a quick description and tell me what it costs.'	'Well, I could do that but I don't believe it would be fair to you. As we have a wide range of facilities, I can't recommend the right one for you until I understand your requirements. You could give me a feel for these at a short meeting at which I can show you how we can help.'

6. Ask questions

While questions are not always necessary, some may be prerequisite to a good meeting, helping with planning and making sure you are 'on target' once you are face-to-face with your prospect. A checklist of questions that may be necessary in your business will be invaluable. One hint, which can often be overlooked, is that if you are visiting the prospect (which they may prefer, particularly for a first meeting) do ask about the location. A sentence or two may save you hours of searching. What about parking? Is there a car park? Similarly, if the prospects are visiting your office make sure they know exactly how to find your property; confirm this in writing (with a map if you have one) and remember to inform others at your office (including the receptionist) as necessary, making sure they know how important the visit is to the firm.

7. *Thanks and confirmation*

At this stage you should summarize briefly what will now happen: 'Right, I will put that brochure in the post to you, Mr Black, and look forward to seeing you, at your office, at 3 p.m. on Monday 27 July.' No more may be required at this stage, though sometimes it is also appropriate to organize written confirmation.

Ringing the prospect to make an appointment can be an awkward kind of call to make: you may well be conscious of the degree of 'push' involved, but a systematic approach will make it easier for you to conduct the call and make it acceptable at the other end.

Next we digress for a moment for a word about letters. These may precede a telephone call and are also more often necessary in reply to a written, or telephone, enquiry.

Letters

Letters last. Unlike telephone calls (which are not often recorded) they stick around to be reread and reconsidered. They need to look neat; think with what trepidation you start reading something that is illegible or untidy. No matter what the subject of the letter is (and sales letters include letters fixing or confirming appointments, introducing yourself, issuing an invitation, even following up after a complaint), you want to be sure that your letters will:

- command attention;
- be understood; and
- be acted upon (it is this last that differentiates persuasive communication from simple factual communication).

If your letters are to do this, you have to take some care in preparing them; in this age of dictating machines and rush and pressure, it is all too easy to just 'dash them off'.

Preparing persuasive (sales) letters

Before you even draft a letter, remember the sequence of persuasion (see Chapter 1), and in particular remember to try to see things through the other person's eyes. Then ask five questions:

- For whom is the letter and its message intended? (This is not always the person to whom it is addressed.)
- What are their particular needs?
- How do our ideas or propositions satisfy those needs – what benefits do they give?
- What do we want the reader to do when he receives the letter? We must have a clear objective for every letter, and these objectives must be clear. (You cannot write the letter, then decide what you want the reader to do; you must write the kind of letter that will best prompt the action you have in mind.)
- How does the reader take this action?

The last two questions are frequently forgotten, but they are very important. It should be perfectly clear in you own mind what you want the recipient to do, and very often this can be put equally clearly to the reader; but having achieved this, you can lose the advantage if lack of information makes it difficult for them to take the action you want.

The most important part of a letter is the first sentence, or possibly the first two. They will determine whether or not the rest of the letter is read. People seldom read a letter in the same sequence in which it was written. Their eyes flick from the sender's address to the ending, then to the greeting and the first sentence, skim to the last and then, if the sender is lucky, back to the first sentence for a more careful reading of the whole letter. So the first sentences contain about the only chance you have of 'holding' the reader, and should arouse immediate interest. But gimmicks should be avoided. They invariably give the reader the impression of being talked down to. So how can we achieve the best opening?

Make sure the start of the letter will:

- command the reader's attention;
- gain their interest; and
- lead easily into the main text.

For example: ask a 'Yes' question; tell them why you are writing to them particularly; tell them why they should read the letter; flatter them (carefully); tell them what they might lose if they ignore the message; give them some 'mind-bending' news (if you have any).

A version of the hackneyed style of first sentence in answer to an enquiry: 'Thank you for your enquiry of (date), I have great pleasure in enclosing . . .' is much used, but unlikely surely to get anyone really sitting up and taking notice. Similarly, why do people start by saying things like 'I am taking this opportunity of sending you . . .' What opportunity, and why should I care? Sorry, I digress, but that is my personal most-hated phrase.

The body of the letter runs straight on from the opening. It must consider the reader's needs or problems from his point of view. It must generate interest. It must get the reader nodding in agreement, 'Yes, I wish you could help me on that'. And of course you are able to help. In drafting you should write down what you intend for the reader and, of course, list the benefits, not features – and in particular the benefits which will help solve that problem and satisfy that need.

You have to anticipate possible objections to your proposition in order to be able to select your strongest benefits and most convincing answers. If there is a need to counter objections, then you may need to make your letter longer and give proof, e.g. something about a third party (the fact that your hotel is used by a notable company, has won an award or is approved by a local association perhaps) selected from the range of such information that should be available. This will reinforce the point and demonstrate that benefits stated are real. However, remember to keep the letter as short as possible. Your aims should be the following: to keep the reader's immediate interest; keep that interest with the best benefit; win him over with a second benefit (or more); obtain action at the end.

In drafting you should make a short summary of the benefits of your proposition. Having decided on what action you want the reader to take, you must be positive about getting it. It is necessary to nudge the reader into action with a decisive final comment or question. Remember too that brochures do not remove the necessity for a good letter. The two must work well together (and some overlap of message is fine), but a good letter is more likely to get read right through than a long brochure – especially if the brochure's text is dull.

The kind of thing I see so often in reply to enquiries leaves a good deal to be desired. Consider the following, a letter I received from a hotel (in one of the major international groups) which I had telephoned to talk with about the possibility of their accommodating a group of people on a scheduled training course.

Dear Mr Forsyth

Following my telephone conversation with you yesterday, I was delighted to hear of your interest in our hotel for a proposed meeting and luncheon some time in the future.

I have pleasure in enclosing for your perusal our banqueting brochure together with the room plan and, as you can see, some of our rooms could prove ideal for your requirements.

At this stage, I would be happy to offer you our delegate rate of … (so much) … to include the following:

- *morning coffee and biscuits;*
- *three-course luncheon with coffee;*
- *afternoon tea with biscuits;*
- *overhead projector and flip chart;*
- *pads and pencils;*
- *room hire;*
- *service and tax;*

and I trust this meets with your approval.

Should you at any time wish to visit our facilities and discuss your particular requirements further, please do not hesitate to contact me but, in the meantime, if you have any queries on the above, I would be pleased to answer them.

Yours sincerely

This is not untypical, and while no doubt well-intentioned, polite and conveying a certain amount of information, does not really begin to sell in an appropriate manner.

Reviewing the content in more detail prompts comments such as:

- I do not wish to know about their delight (of course they want my business); starting with something about me, my need or circumstance would be better.
- I am not running a 'meeting and luncheon', I explained it was a training session – this is their terminology, not mine.
- It is not 'at some time in the future', I quoted a date.
- Next we have more of their pleasure; I am more interested in what receiving the brochure will do for me, rather than what sending it does for them (and, yes, people really do use the word perusal in writing, though it seems very old-fashioned and formal to most – and who would say it?).
- Also, while I approve the room plans (always useful) I do not see this as a banquet and the phrase 'banqueting brochure' does not seem appropriate; again it is their terminology not mine. Incidentally it arrived with a couple of dozen menu suggestions which puts, for me, too much weight on the lunch. It is important, but any hotel that I am likely to run a meeting at will be able to offer a reasonable menu; other considerations come first.
- The section about costs begins 'At this stage . . .' which seems to me to imply 'later we might negotiate something different' although I am sure this is not what is meant. 'I trust this meets with your approval' is old-fashioned office-speak.
- Saying 'Should you at any time wish to visit' hardly takes any initiative. As most people will not book a meeting-room without seeing it, offering to arrange a viewing of the venue, by stating 'You will want to see . . .' and going on to make an arrangement to do so might be better.
- As 'queries' implies omissions, something left out or unclear, an offer of additional information makes better sense; what is actually said casts doubt.

The total impression is of a standard letter, one that goes out to many enquirers. What customers want is something that is manifestly for them, tailored to their enquiry, relating to what they said or wrote, and talking in their terms.

This is a real opportunity area.

Have a look at what has been going out of your office recently. If it is standard, introspective, in a rut, try a new approach; given the prevailing standards you may find it an easy way to stand out positively.

When I show and review such a letter on courses, participants usually agree the inadequacies of such writing; they are also quick to say something like 'If you are so clever, what do you write?' Fair enough. The letter that follows is a redraft of the one critiqued a little earlier. It may not be the definitive 'right' letter – but I am sure it is better than the earlier one. What matters is less that you find and follow some standard 'good example'; more that you take a considered and creative approach, write in terms that clients can identify with, and create a positive impact.

Dear Mr Forsyth

Training Seminar: venue arrangements to make your meeting succeed

Your training seminar would, I am sure, go well here. Let me explain why. From how you describe the event, you need a business-like environment, no distractions, all the necessary equipment and everything the venue does to work like clockwork.

Our xxx room is among a number regularly successfully used for this kind of meeting. It is currently free on the dates you mentioned: 3/4 June. As an example, one package that suits many organizers is:

- *morning tea/coffee with tasty pastries or biscuits;*

- *three-course lunch with tea/coffee;*

- *afternoon tea/coffee and refreshments;*

- *pads, pencils and name cards for each participant;*

- *room hire (including the use of an OHP and flipchart) at a cost of £xxx per head, including service and tax.*

Alternatively, we could discuss other options; our main concern is to meet your specific needs and get every detail just right.

You will almost certainly want to see the room suggested. Perhaps I may telephone to set up a convenient time for you to come in and have a look around. In the meantime, our meetings brochure is enclosed (the room mentioned is illustrated on page 4). This, and the room plans enclosed with it, will enable you to begin to plan how your meeting would work here.

Thank you for thinking of us; I look forward to speaking to you again soon.

Yours sincerely

Note: this is surely more customer-focused, starts with a description most meeting organizers are likely to nod to, and is – intentionally – less formally, almost more conversationally, worded.

What next? Well, if we are optimistic, we will assume that the prospect says 'Yes' to a meeting, so the next thing is to plan the meeting.

4 The power of preparation: creating an initial edge

ALREADY, a phrase like 'It does not just happen' has appeared more than once in this text. If it is repeated it is because it is an important fact to take on board. The best salespeople in my experience do not operate off the top of their heads, though they may make it look as if they do. Instead, they worry about their homework and do it systematically. Yet in many industries, preparation for selling is skimped and sales meetings go less well as a result. In hotels, where many prospects meet you in the property, and where the better the property the greater the chances of thinking that it speaks for itself, the dangers of neglecting preparation are perhaps greater than in other fields.

Preparation may consist of just a few moments thought immediately before the prospect arrives. Or it may mean sitting round the table with a colleague for an hour or more thrashing out the best way to deal with a particular client. But, whether it takes a long or short time, it must always happen. Consider what must be done and how each area can help the subsequent meeting go more smoothly and successfully for you.

Records and research

Before doing anything else, consider who it is you are going to see. If this is someone new to you, such consideration will start with the details from an enquiry, or, if it is a new contact, from whatever details led you to contact them. The information that will be useful has already been considered in Chapter 3. Suffice it to say, there is a minimum amount of information that one should have when meeting a prospect, and if it takes a little research to obtain this, so be it. A few telephone calls, or a few minutes with a good trade directory, may make all the difference to how well informed you appear at the meeting, and the useful information you have forms the basis for planning the kind of meeting you wish to conduct. If you regularly deal with people from certain specialized industries, it may be worth subscribing to and reading regularly the trade journals of that field. In this way, when a new company makes contact, you may already know a little about them and the world in which they operate.

But what about past customers? Start with customer records. They are a chore to keep up, but they do help. Don't delude yourself by believing that you can hold every detail of every client and contact in your head. None of us can. Records need to be clear, up-to-date and should make good sense to anyone else who has to take over from us in an emergency (this is an important point: they are the corporate records, not your records, and anyone who has taken over from someone else and found a mess will readily agree the importance). They should list information about the organization, about the contacts, their needs, past usage, business potential and more; formats vary from company to company; one example of a record used in the industry, suitable for prospects or ongoing contacts, appears in Figure 4.1.

The important thing is that it gives you the information you want. In some establishments, the basis of the records is old. At worst it was originated in simpler times and no longer serves the present purpose well. If this is the case for you, then the form itself must be changed. This may be difficult. Management may need persuading, a new form will need designing and its content agreed upon. The job of updating what may be several hundred cards is also itself daunting (though it can be done progressively). But it is vital to have a workable system. Many such systems are these days on computer. This is excellent if the system is good, though it may make it more difficult to change. Assuming that consulting the records yields useful information, plan what you will do at the forthcoming meeting, by setting clear objectives.

	Contact	Position	Ref:	Name:				
1			Type of business:	Address:				
2								
Potential use:								
Competitor info:				Telephone:		Fax:		

	Date	Call type: Cold call	Enquiry	Regular	Call summary	Products/Facilities* A	B	C	Next action
O									
O									

Figure 4.1: Example of customer/prospect record card (back-up information can be recorded on the reverse side)
A = Conference business; B = bedrooms etc. as suits each individual property

Setting clear objectives

Every sales meeting needs clear objectives; if you do not have a clear idea of what you are trying to achieve, it is difficult to begin achieving it. Objectives aid the thinking that precedes each meeting, and assist us in staying on course during the meeting. The overall objective 'to sell' is just too vague to be helpful; there may be many different things you aim to achieve, either singly or together. As business tends not to automatically come from one meeting, but often involves a chain of events, this makes setting objectives even more important. You may start by saying (of a telephone call, for example) that it is to persuade them to accept a brochure, then move on to objectives that focus on getting them in to see the property, prompting them to make a provisional booking for something, or confirming that one booking and ending by seeking to establish a regular arrangement. The permutations are varied. We will review the details of the process with an example in mind, and start from the well-known maxim that objectives must be SMART. That is:

Specific: setting out clearly what you intend. Assume that you are seeing the training manager of a medium-sized local company with a view to selling primarily meeting-room space. Then a specific objective might be to get him to book one (or two) events to test you out. This might well be appropriate at the stage when he had agreed to visit you and inspect the place, though earlier a specific objective might have been to set up that visit.

Measurable: both the objectives mentioned above can easily be measured. The prospect either agrees to meet or makes the test booking or does not; you know quite clearly whether you have achieved what you set out to do. Conversely, an objective such as wanting to 'increase their awareness of us' is difficult to measure in the same kind of way.

Achievable: this means asking if the objective is reasonable given the circumstances, or just pie in the sky. To say, of our example, that we will aim to book all his future training meetings from now on is not likely to be something that we can actually do: whereas the test booking makes much more sense viewed from the customer's perspective if we are really being practical and aiming for something that stands a real chance of obtaining agreement. Aim high by all means, but be circumspect to some extent too.

Realistic: here we are concerned with whether we *should* do it. If the test booking he wants is on the same day as another meeting, perhaps the other is with one of his competitors or will be very noisy; then maybe we should aim for something else. A clash of this sort might end with the new customer never likely to rebook a venue.

Timed: here we refer to when something can be done. Training meetings tend to be arranged some time ahead, so looking to book something in the next week might be inappropriate, whereas something within three months makes good sense. Timing is always important, you also have to decide for how long to pursue things. When clients say 'Not at the moment' or 'I am too busy to visit you' they may mean just that (and not that they are trying to avoid you). Some events have long lead times, weeks, months, sometimes years, especially for something like an annual conference. Persistence pays off and some of the business goes to those who are prepared to keep in touch when their competitors lose heart, or find that they cannot get over the embarrassment of what they see as 'yet another follow-up'.

Clear objectives keep you on track and let you come over to the customer as someone who thinks through what they are doing, and this in turn makes an impression as part of their need to anticipate service standards before use.

Having done any necessary research and thought through the question of objectives, you can then consider the nature of the meeting you wish to run, in order to achieve them. Of course, it would be neither practical nor desirable to script the meeting and attempt to plan it down to the last word. On the other hand, only one person can direct a meeting at one time, and in selling, you should always aim at being the one in the driving seat. I use the word 'direct' advisably. You may direct and direct firmly, yet not do most of the talking, or be seen to be taking a lead (unless you want to) and certainly without appearing pushy or inappropriate.

In order to direct, you need a clear plan, one that acts like a route map and helps keep you from veering away from the ideal route as might otherwise be the case. Of course, you never know exactly what the other's response will be and all customers are in any case different, so keeping close to track is the best that you can hope for. Without a plan, any course correction is impossible. To suggest an analogy, it is rather like the helmsman of a sailing ship, who might take a number of courses depending on the wind and weather – the course plotted on his chart helps him stay close to where he is ideally heading. Figure 4.2 shows this concept graphically.

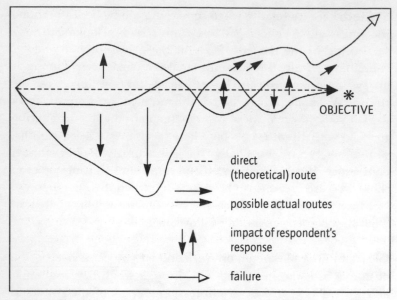

Figure 4.2: Structuring and directing the communication towards our objective

It is useful to keep this sort of picture in mind as you plan and direct your meetings. Think through each meeting, asking yourself such questions as:

- How will you start?
- What references back to prior meetings or research are necessary?
- What questions do you need to ask, and how?
- How can you give the right initial impression and begin to build rapport?
- What are you going to tell them? – certainly the key points can be planned.
- What are you *not* going to tell them? – pressure of time means you usually must be selective.
- What are you going to show them? (more of this later).
- How are you going to conclude, bearing in mind the commitment you want?

Realistically, the early part is more easily planned than the latter part – when more interaction makes its course less predictable. We now turn to some of the 'weather' coming directly from the customer that will act negatively to change the course of events.

Anticipating objections

Objections are a natural reaction to the sales process (something we investigate further in Chapter 6). And, while customers are all different and you no doubt have to deal with a number of different types of people – a secretary one minute, a managing director the next – experience does illustrate common factors and there is no excuse for allowing what you should see as routine matters catch you out. For example, if your main conference room has pillars in it, some customers are going to object: 'I don't think we could get the layout we want with these pillars'. Similarly, if your restaurant closes too early, or your bedrooms do not have the equipment needed to make hot drinks or there is no swimming pool, then you will get objections to these points.

Occasionally you will be asked something that has never, or rarely, cropped up before and this may be thrown at you. But for the most part the objections are predictable, cropping up all too regularly. You may not know how an individual customer will raise a point and the possibilities are almost infinite, but there is an area here where some preparation is only sensible and will help you run a smoother meeting. How do you handle the question of the pillars or whatever else you find you need to deal with when discussing your own venue? Some thought in this area can very easily pay dividends, and certainly being apparently caught out of even being indecisive about something the customer will expect you to deal with ten times a day, gives very much the wrong impression.

Sales aids

A sales aid refers to either an item, place or person that can be used to better explain, demonstrate or describe something during the meeting. Such things are especially important in venues, where as well as individual things, the whole establishment can act as an aid to help you sell. Or it should do.

On some of the many inspection visits I have made, something along the following lines has occurred. I am touring the hotel with one of the salespeople, all is going well, they seem professional, more important they seem to have a clear understanding of what I want and the establishment itself is, certainly at first sight, impressive. We go through the building and head towards a particular meeting-room, one described as ideal for my purposes. At the end of a long corridor we arrive at the meeting-room door – and it is locked. A look of blank amazement is followed by the obvious remark 'I am afraid it seems to be locked', and they disappear to get the key, leaving me to while away what seems like an interminable length of time in an empty corridor. At worst they return ten minutes later full of apologies, open the door and discover they have no idea where the light switches are located. Then, having located and switched on the lights, we find they illuminate what looks like a bomb site – the remains of the dinner held on the previous evening.

It is important to recognize just how off-putting this sort of occurrence is for the customer. All the disasters catalogued above may not occur on the same occasion, but something like it happens much more often than you might think; and even small hiccups can have a disproportionate negative impact. Why does this sort of thing happen? Because no one worried about preparation.

Such things need arranging, they need checking – only when they go smoothly will they help build the image you want and play an active part in making the whole meeting or 'show-round' go well. Let me take you through more examples to show how this area should work, starting with things and then moving on to people.

Illustrations

A heading that should be taken to include brochures, pictures, room plans, menus, wine lists and the like. Most hotels do not have anything like enough examples to show in this sort of form. To understand the importance, consider two different points of view. You are intimately familiar with your property, its facilities and the many ways in which it can be used. You can look at the Reception area and imagine it fully staffed to handle quickly and efficiently the arrival of a large group; you can look at a meeting-room and imagine it set out for a wedding, with flowers and all the trimmings. Or a meeting-room set out boardroom style or in a U-shape. Customers cannot do this; or they certainly cannot do it anything like as well as you can. Few of them have the necessary experience that would make it possible.

Never assume too much about your customer's imagination.

In selling, it is your job to spell things out to them, to paint a picture for them. And sales aids should help make this possible; they should make it easy. Yet in many hotels, for example, they do not have any photographs of the hotel with anything happening in it. Pictures of empty reception areas, empty bedrooms and empty meeting-rooms (you can always spot the brochures that were produced as the hotel originally opened by the photographs that have only the same two people – usually the sales manager and his secretary – in every picture).

To sell effectively you need a good selection of this sort of thing; a meeting-room, for example, might have a dozen pictures of it in different guises – a business meeting, a wedding, a cocktail party. Room plans work best if you can cover them with tracing paper and actually plan out with the customer what the best layout will be.

Not only must you have the right things, they must be well and flexibly stored. You may need to show things in a different order to different customers, and you certainly need to be able to find them and be sure they are in pristine condition. Wherever the meeting takes place, the customer must find these things appear as if by magic; from your briefcase in his office, your folder in your office, and during the tour-round as well if appropriate, when things have to be organized so that you can manage them effectively as you walk around.

The establishment

Every aspect of the hotel itself is a potential aid to selling (and a few will make it more difficult). Again, preparation is necessary, as we saw above in the example of the lost key. You need to know a whole range of things:

- which rooms are occupied or empty (and tidy or untidy) – and this is true of bedrooms and meeting-rooms;
- what times different areas are accessible (when will a meeting be taking its coffee break; when will a corridor be in a mess as rooms are made up?);
- which areas are impressive (and where needs decorating or is currently being decorated).

Again there are many things to think about and check if the right impression is to be made; and the same principles apply to people.

People

You need to be well turned out, of course, but there may be other staff who may be seen as a customer visits your property. On many occasions I have approached a hotel's Reception, having made an appointment to see one of the sales staff, and on asking for them by name the reply is 'Who?' This is compounded by some who go on to make it clear that they are not even aware of a sales department, much less understand anything about it.

On another occasion – one I will never forget – I was sitting in discussion with a hotel sales manager in a public lounge area of the hotel. As we talked, a cleaner came into the room at the end furthest from us and began to work her way down the room with a vacuum cleaner. It got nearer and nearer till she asked me, quite politely, to move my feet so that she could clean the area beneath! She then disappeared from the room and the sales manager did not so much as pause, much less comment on this happening. Incidents like this occur all too often and serve to illustrate the lack of preparation.

There is no excuse for not advising Reception of when customers or potential customers are coming and perhaps also briefing them as to how they can help make the time spent in the hotel really impressive. It is simple enough, and which customer does not like to be greeted by name and have it made clear he is expected and that staff are pleased to have him visit?

The same goes for a range of people that you may meet and interact with as you are in the hotel with a customer: the receptionist, doorman, restaurant staff and banqueting staff. The same applies to senior staff (more senior than you) and even to other customers; for example, if you plan to show a prospect around a meeting-room when the users are at coffee, you need to ask them; but do remember that they may arrive back while you are still in the room.

Preparations for the show-round are so important that some establishments have a checklist to help them ensure that all is ready and will go well (Figure 4.3 summarizes what is necessary for the preparation of a sales meeting).

Everything that has been mentioned here makes a further point. Preparation does not just involve thinking about things in advance – though it may be characterized by the old adage that one should always engage the brain before the mouth – it often necessitates making some notes. During a sales meeting you will probably have a file with you, or a clipboard, something to keep brochures, photos, etc. together, so a few written notes relating to your objectives and plan of action will not be noticed by the customer. But their absence may be noticeable if the meeting is in any way disjointed or ineffective, and they can be of real practical use in making things go well.

Selling is never easy in a competitive business, and we are discussing a *very* competitive business. It is not made any easier if there is a lack of attention to detail. It was the hair-stylist Vidal Sassoon who was credited with saying: 'The only place where success comes before work is in the dictionary'; and he is right.

A little effort spent before a sales meeting is time very well spent. Preparation is one of the first things that can give you a real 'edge' on competition. It is easy to imagine a customer comparing two rather similar places, where often nothing differentiates one from another, being somewhat more impressed simply by the way in which all these kinds of factor are handled. The people – and you in particular – and how they go about things may, quite simply, be the greatest single differentiating factor in some decisions.

The next thing to consider further, therefore, and one that

goes closely with everything discussed here, is the salespeople themselves: the impression they give and whether it is in accord with the kind of approach – and service – which prospects and customers want. This is the first subject of the next chapter, after which we can turn to how all factors can contribute to making an interactive face-to-face meeting more persuasive.

When planning for sales meetings with potential clients who are not already known to us, it is crucial to devote enough time to research. Pre-meeting desk research should cover information about:

- ❏ The person to be seen.
- ❏ Customer's company/industry.
- ❏ Purchase influencers.
- ❏ The competition.
- ❏ Possible needs and future plans.
- ❏ The sales potential for us.
- ❏ Travel arrangements, etc.

Research into the client and his situation is an ongoing process which should be continued into the sales meeting to include finding out:

- ❏ Who the decision-makers are.
- ❏ Any preferred buying or approvals systems.
- ❏ The client's needs in more detail.
- ❏ Preferred call frequency for future reference.
- ❏ Future plans.

Planning for the meeting itself
The opening
Plan your opening so that you will be able to:

Figure 4.3: Preparation checklist

❏ Put your client at ease.
❏ Get him interested and talking.
❏ Explore his needs.
❏ Establish his priorities.

The main presentation of your ideas/proposals
Plan your presentation so that you will be able to:

❏ Offer your client desirable results from his point of view.
❏ Prove your case to his satisfaction.
❏ Explain complex points simply.
❏ Show how his needs can be met (and demonstrate during any show-round).

Objections
Plan thoroughly so that:

❏ You have considered what they might be.
❏ You have got answers which will satisfy him.
❏ Your answers are related to his needs.

The close
Plan your close so that:

❏ You get a commitment (to book or move to the next stage).
❏ You meet your objectives.
❏ You make it easy for him to agree.
❏ Leave him feeling better than before the meeting.

Support material
This is a vital area in the planning and preparation stages because, as well as showing things, you can actually quote examples which relate to your client's needs.

Figure 4.3: Preparation checklist (continued)

You should:

- ❏ Identify what you need to take along to the meeting.
- ❏ Identify what the customer may need.
- ❏ Ensure availability of items to take.
- ❏ Decide on the best method of presentation.
- ❏ Work out beforehand what the benefits are to the client of each point made/shown.
- ❏ And that you think through how you will handle the show-round.

Figure 4.3: Preparation checklist (continued)

5 Face to face: conducting a persuasive meeting

AFTER what may seem a great many preliminaries, prospecting, preparing, telephoning and letter-writing, the moment finally arrives when you are face-to-face with the prospect. The meeting can occur in a variety of circumstances and the following are worth investigating first before going into the detail of the meeting itself and how to conduct it.

Where to meet?

There are two main options which can perhaps be summed up in the immortal phrase 'Your place or mine?' Without a doubt it is always better to get the prospect to come to you. This has the obvious and considerable advantage that they will then see the property. In addition, it has important advantages for your productivity. Quite simply you are likely to be able to find time to see more people if they come to you than if you spend a great deal of time in the car going to them. And, all other things being equal, if you see more people, you will sell more business.

A word about visiting people. Some hotel salespeople are reluctant to visit others, recognizing perhaps that it is more difficult to do a thorough job away from the hotel. On the other hand some clients prefer that you visit them; others will demand it as a first step. They are not only busy people, but they have very many more important things to do than select venues; this is something, incidentally, always worth keeping in mind, though we are prone to think that our property is the most important thing in the world. What some may well prefer is to talk to a short list of representatives from venues that seem to meet their requirements, and then only see those that impress. So, if this is what they want, then this is what they should get; you can miss good prospects by avoiding meetings of this sort.

If, on the other hand, they are willing to come to you then you must think about how such a meeting is best set up; some of the questions have been mentioned before:

- Who needs briefing about the visit?
- When is the best time to see them?

You also need to think about where you should see them and in what order to do things. If you start at Reception, do you do a tour first, then sit down and discuss matters or vice versa? And where do you sit? Do you have an office; if not, is there somewhere businesslike you can conduct the meeting, somewhere the client will feel comfortable? This all needs thinking about. Some venues have what might be called an 'inherited norm'; in other words the salesperson conducts the meeting in the way they were trained to do, and that way was what someone else was shown even earlier. Sometimes you find that it is years since anyone actually thought about what made best sense for the client (it is not just a matter of what suits you best) and meetings continue on the basis of the blind leading the blind (or perhaps the bland leading the bland, as such an approach makes for a dull experience for clients). Generally speaking, you are likely to need some talk and discussion first, before showing the clients around.

As we explore the sequence of events of a meeting the logic of holding a discussion first will become clear. The intention in this chapter is to review the techniques you can deploy during a meeting without concerning yourselves too much with what sort of meeting it is, i.e. on their territory, or yours, on a tour around the property or whatever. We will start, logically, with general principles. *Note:* comments about the important area of the 'show-round' are added separately towards the end of this chapter.

The sales process

In the first chapter the seven classic stages of the buying-decision-making process were listed (see Figure 1.3 on page 9). Here we relate the various stages involved to the four main stages of the face-to-face meeting; that is:

- opening the sale;
- presenting the case;
- handling objections; and
- closing.

This structure provides the real route map. What has to be borne in mind here is not a fixed way forward, but a structure and approach which will guide the way through the conversation, enabling the salesperson to maintain the initiative, direct the proceedings and yet make what is going on entirely acceptable to the client or the prospect.

The route map analogy is a good one. You have to keep the full picture in front of you and, even if selecting different choices along the route, keep moving in the right direction. In addition, the fine detail is important; miss one signpost and you are off the route and may perhaps become lost.

Similarly, the detail is important here, as we move through the four stages. Small – perhaps seemingly basic – details are as important to the success of the whole encounter as the big issues.

The first stage is, of course, the opening. This is, as we shall see, a little more than just a series of introductory exchanges; it sets the scene for the whole meeting and has a considerable impact on its outcome.

1. Opening the sale

It is a funny thing about meetings; you may have noticed that they have two beginnings. One is ritual. It is concerned with the initial remarks such as 'Good morning', and also 'Did you find our offices OK?', 'What a dreadful day, nothing but rain the whole summer' (so what else is new?). Remarks such as these allow us to get into the swing of things. Then, someone, often the buyer, says something like, 'Right, what I suggest we do this morning is . . .', and the meeting starts again. You know the feeling.

This area is worthy of consideration, but with care we are, after all, only talking about a minute or two and must not get ridiculously psychological about it (certainly it takes longer to review the process than for it to actually happen). But it is important. You want to run and direct the meeting. Not in an unpleasant sense from the point of view of the customer; the trick is to *run the kind of meeting you want, and the customer finds he likes* (and preferably likes more than any meetings he has with your competitors). Only one person can effectively be 'in charge'. There is a line in Shakespeare's *Much Ado About Nothing* that says that when 'two men ride on a horse, one must ride behind'. This certainly makes the point. If the sales person does not get hold of the meeting, the customer surely will. So, what can we do about this?

The answer lies in those first, ritual moments. Unless the initiative is taken then, it may not be possible for you to take control for some time; at worst it will be completely lost. Specifically, this means keeping the conversation off the weather or whatever, and contributing something more businesslike which still fulfils the ritual process. The two tactics outlined below make good examples.

Appeal to pride
When using this tactic you comment on something positive about the customer's business. This could be simply an observation of how smart their new reception area looks, 'I'm sure it impresses all your customers', or may come from your research, 'I noticed in last week's trade papers how successful you have been with the export initiative in Germany'. Good research will mean you know your customer will be able to say, 'Yes, I'm very pleased about that'. This kind of comment shows an interest. It shows you have done some checking and it provides a ritual moment of relevant conversation.

Good turns

This approach is very effective with people you see regularly. A good exponent of the 'good turn' approach is a salesman who comes to see me regularly. He notes the kind of work I do, the kind of industries I work in and will often arrive with, say, a magazine article in his briefcase. 'I know you do a lot in the hotel and travel industry,' he might say, 'I wondered if you had seen this?' Seen it or not, I like the approach and it often produces something interesting. It costs him, of course, nothing except a little time and attention.

Many similar actions can be taken and then the salesperson can move on to say 'Let's get down to business', from which control of the meeting follows more naturally.

At the same time the beginning of the opening should flow through a structure, if only to avoid starting with the trite phrases of the less professional salesperson: 'I just happened to be passing'; 'How's business?' and so on.

Having initiated the meeting in a way that will appear interesting and businesslike to the client and having gained control of it in terms of direction, you can move on to a number of other things that need to be happening during the opening minutes of the meeting.

The key issues are to:

- create and then maintain interest;
- make the client feel they are being dealt with in a way that recognizes their importance and that they have unique individual needs which are being looked into;
- demonstrate that you are not only expert in your field of work, but also understanding;
- actively discover the client's needs (with more details than may well be volunteered), and use the knowledge in a way that enables you to move on to making a case for your own property and its services.

These are clearly issues which have implications throughout the meeting, but, as the old saying has it: *first impressions last* and it is very important to get off to a good start. 'Good' means that the client finds what you are doing is right for them (as well as being persuasive to meet your own objectives). In fact, this means that the meeting needs to make good initial impact on a businesslike basis and that you need to make an appropriate and lasting personal impression; remember that the actual purchase may be a few stages down the line and that before people will buy from you, they have to remember you.

*   *   *

Note: A short digression may be useful here to make a point about business cards. First, consider a point about customers. It may be difficult to believe, but people, particularly those who make regular use of hotels, do have difficulty in remembering you and your hotel. Regularly I hear, and participate in, this kind of conversation: 'You know the conference we had last year in Oxford – the thing for all the distributors?'

'Er, yes.'

'What was the hotel where we ran it called?'

'Oh . . . no, can't think of it, but wasn't it part of a group?'

'No, surely not, it was . . .' and so on, often reaching no conclusion. Personally I know I often thumb through a pile of business cards and cannot place which is the hotel I want to go back to. If you find this difficult to believe, be careful. What is important to people is the trip, the meeting, the conference and what happened at it; where it took place is not anything like as likely to be remembered.

I have seen a number of business cards over the years which have a picture of the property on them, sometimes a line drawing, one in four-colour print. These I can always place. The colour one brings back a vivid impression; I can remember walking into Reception and what it was like, I can remember the meeting-room (I was there to conduct a course) and, as it all went well, I would certainly go back there. On second thoughts, this is not digression, it is an important point, one which can help make sure you are remembered.

*   *   *

Back to the early part of the meeting. The detail, especially early on, may be important. Always be polite, do not desert all the formalities, even with people you have got to know well; it is after all a business relationship. You need:

- a greeting;
- to make clear, sometimes, why you are seeing them (if you have initiated the contact and are not responding to an enquiry);
- to move the meeting into a phase during which you can easily and promptly find out more about the clients, and the needs they have; an initial question or two may position this stage (though it may well be worth actually spelling out the need for some questions: 'If you can bear with me while I check a few details, then we can see whether we can offer something that will . . .').

In addition, with continuing contacts you may need to check for or pick up on any outstanding issues; in other words, points that link through from previous meetings or contacts.

The greeting
Obviously, your greeting must be right for the time of day, but also for the depth of your relationship and your customer's/ prospect's personality type. This means that even long-standing customers can still expect a formal greeting, whereas some prospects respond well to an informal greeting. If in any doubt, take the formal route.

The question of whether and when to use first names can only be answered within the context of what your company recommends and what each contact finds acceptable. First-name use is more common now, but if in doubt remain more, rather than less, formal; certainly until there are clear signs from the other party.

To make it just a little more likely that you will be remembered (after all, the prospect may see many different sales people), when it comes to introducing yourself it is best to use both your names – John Smith – and, at the same time, hand over a business card if you are meeting for the first time. (This is very much a ritual in some parts of the world: the Japanese even have waterproof plastic cards to use by the hotel pool!)

The interest-creating comment

There are two reasons for including in your opening words an interest-creating comment:

- to demonstrate your knowledge of and interest in your customer's/prospect's industry, company, people, plans, policies, etc.;
- to begin the process of raising the contact's interest in and level of receptivity to you and what you are there for.

The reason for calling

This must be expressed as buyer benefit. If a relationship already exists between you and a customer, you should be able to easily devise a highly relevant benefit; if there is no relationship, you must choose a benefit which experience tells you that most customers have found valuable. For instance, with a regular customer the objective may be linked to selling the range, introducing aspects of the property someone has not, as yet, tried. Someone who likes your facilities for, say, business meetings, and finds them good value, may be interested in a similar arrangement for social functions. A cost-effective solution for these other arrangements becomes the benefit.

The customer is not likely to be interested in buying more of the range simply because he likes you, whichever customer you approach.

A check for outstanding issues

In certain other industries, for example book publishing or health care, it is common practice for a supplier to take back unsold products. It may well be the best approach to encourage a customer to raise this, or other such outstanding matters, before you begin your current presentation. This helps 'clear the decks'.

If your customer's priority need is to resolve a problem concerning, say, a previous invoice, then this will be in the forefront of his or her mind. Until this need is satisfied he or she will not be receptive to the idea of buying anything more.

In such a case, helping your customer at the outset of an

interview may give you some sort of minor bargaining chip; their
initial view of you is then more positive.

The first fact-finding question

This is the bridge which links the interview opening with the
interview proper. Your question should relate to the interest-
creating comment and your reason for calling.

The following examples illustrate the four parts of an opening
in action:

Example 1

Greeting

'Good afternoon, Mr James. I'm Susan Smith. Thank you for
coming to see us. I know you are busy so I will make sure you are
on your way from here in an hour or so.'

Interest-generating comment

'I know last week's conference went well, your assistant said the
feedback from those attending was very positive. I hope this will
have a positive effect on your business.'

Reason for meeting

'That was a one-off event, of course, perhaps we can explore how
we can help with the regular meetings your training department
is concerned with.'

First fact-finding question

'Perhaps you can tell me a little more about them; how many are
there planned for the next six months?'

Example 2

Greeting

'Hello John, good to see you again.'

Interest-generating comment

'I know you are busy with your planning period at this time of
year, that and the budgeting must be a bit of a chore coming
during your peak sales season.'

Reason for meeting
'That's why I thought it was worth meeting now, though, if we can agree a basis for your use of the hotel during the whole of the coming year, I may be able to show you some savings which will go well into those budgets.'

First fact-finding question
'Do you see the volume of business increasing next year?'

Whether it is a first meeting or one of a regular series, or whether it is at the hotel or at the client's office, this kind of sequence will help get things off on the right foot. It is a stage that deserves a little thought in preparation; indeed you ought to appear prepared and come across as interested to talk about what they want or are likely to find of interest. Of course, you are not trying to settle on a standard routine here; rather, find just the right start for each person you see, one that matches them and their situation. Another technique that helps at this stage (and indeed others) is what is most often called 'signposting'. This simply flags ahead what you are aiming at, or suggesting covering. For example, you might say: 'Let me start by checking how you felt about the arrangements for the function you held here last week, then we can discuss your plans for the coming period and see if there are any ways in which we could help reduce costs for you.' If the client agrees this, tacitly or otherwise it sets the scene for what comes next – you can in fact then work through what is agreed.

All sorts of meeting formats are valid. I was invited and attended a lunch recently at a hotel with eight people including the sales executive, three past clients, four new contacts. The group was well mixed, the conversation was stimulating, and the salesperson carefully included elements that were very much the 'sales pitch' and succeeded in making the whole event pleasant and interesting. It made an impact and will no doubt provide a springboard for follow-up action. This idea will not, of course, be right for everyone. It does, however, demonstrate the right kind of thinking; such an approach may prompt other ideas.

Other approaches are more generally applicable. Suggesting, for example, an agenda can help you get hold of the meeting – an agenda that suits you, but also makes sense to the customer, and is phrased carefully: 'It might be most helpful to you, Mr Customer, if we were to take . . . first, then . . .' This is a good example of sales technique which, to the customer, appears helpful and focuses on their needs. They are at liberty to amend your suggestion, but you are both likely to end up following broadly your suggestion.

Having made a good start, there is still a great deal that should go on in the stages of the sale. Perhaps the most important is concerned with finding out about customers, and their needs.

Identification of customer needs

Successful selling is particularly dependent on this stage in the buying process being well handled. Exploring, identifying and agreeing to the client's needs correctly make him want to hear your proposition. Subsequently, making it attractive reduces the possibility of objections and thus obtains more voluntary commitments.

Remember – people act to relieve actual needs they feel. Where the need is low, the solution has a low impact; where the need is high, the solution has a high impact, either positively or negatively depending on the way it is offered. Sometimes, clients will volunteer their needs and priorities. More often, needs have to be explored and identified before they can be agreed on and priorities set. Even comparatively small points of information can prove very useful as the meeting progresses. For example, simply finding out that the topic of a meeting is confidential can change the way you then talk about the meeting-room you recommend, the layout and other arrangements – all of which are linked back to the fact of confidentiality.

Exploration can be done using either questions or statements or by a combination of both questions *and* statements. Questions are initially safer and more productive, but they have to be carefully and correctly used.

Questioning techniques

The first rule is to make sure questions are asked in a way which is clear, and not ambiguous.

The following (an apocryphal story from the world of market research questionnaires) makes the point: Ask people 'Are you in favour of smoking while praying?', and most people will say 'No'. Ask 'Are you in favour of praying while smoking?' and most people will say 'Yes'. Yet the question is actually describing the same thing – the two activities being undertaken simultaneously. So phrase what you ask with real precision.

Secondly, one must be conscious of the various types of questions and how they are best used. The main ones are:

1. Open questions

Usually commencing What?, Where?, When?, Who?, How?, Why?, these cannot be answered simply with a 'Yes' or 'No', and this prompts a fuller answer and maintains the flow of conversation.

Example: 'Tell me, what kind of people will be attending?'

2. Closed questions

More likely to commence with something along the lines of: 'Do you . . . ?', these can be answered simply with a 'Yes' or 'No'; indeed they encourage this to happen.

Example: 'Is it a management meeting?'

They have their dangers, and do not encourage conversation, and are useful in confirming roles, though they do not produce so much, or such precise information as open questions.

3. Rhetorical questions

These are questions which either contain the answer within them, or to which a spoken answer may not or need not be given.

In fact, no response can usually be taken as acceptance.

Example: 'With these arrangements, I expect you will want the coffee served at the back of the meeting-room, won't you?'

4. Directed questions

These contain within their phraseology almost a description of how the answer should be phrased; they are a particular phrasing of open questions.

Example: 'Would you please tell me how important you see the leisure facilities being?'

It is very important to know not only *what* your clients want, but *why* they want it – and to understand the circumstances from their point of view.

Consider for a moment: what does someone mean when they say about a meeting: '. . . it is a product briefing session?' It is not, in fact, very clear. It is what might be called *background information*. If we are to be seen as better informed than our competitors then we must get beyond this level of information. This has implications for the questioning techniques touched on earlier. Here, we will concern ourselves with a technique of questioning designed specifically to discover people's real intentions, feelings and requirements. It is described by the term *probing questions*. These are, in other words, a sequence of questions focusing on, and building on the same issues – 'digging' for information.

These questions are most often defined as proceeding through four stages:

- *Background* questions give you basic information from which you can begin to draw conclusions.
- *Problem* questions begin to focus on the other person's situation.
- *Effect* questions help focus on what is happening as a result of the prevailing situation.
- *Need* questions get the person to state needs in their terms.

The sequence that follows, while not exactly representing real life, makes the sequence clear:

'Where are you?'
'Up to my neck in the river.'
'Does this pose any problem?'
'Yes, I can't swim.'
'So what will happen if you stay there?'
'I shall probably drown.'
'Do you want me to pull you out?'
'Yes, please.'

The first answer poses as many questions as it answers – maybe it is a hot day and the person is swimming. The last question prompts an entirely specific response and puts the person selling the rope from the bank in a powerfully persuasive position!

Now consider one of the questions posed a moment ago:

'What kind of meeting is it?' That prompted the answer: 'It's a product briefing session.' This tells us something, but not very much. (It could, of course, be worse; they might have said 'a staff meeting' or even just 'residential meeting'.) Some intelligent follow-up questioning, however, will give us a good deal more.

Ask 'What kind of meeting is it' and they say 'It's a product briefing session.' A supplementary question or two adds to the picture:

'What kind of people will be attending?'

'They are the principals of all our main overseas dealerships.'

'And what kind of briefing is it?'

'Well, it's the first stage of a new product launch, I mustn't say more at present.'

Both the above are background questions. Now a problem question (these do not have to contain the word 'problem' – it may refer to positive factors but must focus on client concerns) will tell us more:

'Sounds important – you will want everything to go just right won't you? Tell me more about it.'

'Yes, it's the first step to launching a major new product. So, yes, it would be disastrous if anything went wrong.'

So far all these are open questions. Next, perhaps as we make certain inferences about implications, a closed question focuses the issue best:

'So, with senior people from all over the world, able to make a major impact on your sales, you are not only going to want to be sure the event goes well, but that it creates the right impression, aren't you?'

'Very much so, it will be the most important meeting of the year, that's for sure.'

The client here is talking about what are for them important details, so there is normally no problem in prompting this degree of information which they are, in fact, pleased to discuss. If a question such as 'What kind of meeting is it?' proves to be simply facilities-orientated, it is seen as (no doubt efficient) checking. If your questions appear not only practical, but also prove your interest in their meeting and making it successful, then the impact is greater – and more likely to differentiate you from less creative competitors.

Throughout the process, open or closed questions can be equally useful, but open questions (that cannot be answered with a 'Yes' or 'No') encourage the client to talk and so produce more information.

The type and combination of questions asked is very important. Experience shows that asking fewer background questions but focusing them better, asking more problem questions, asking implications questions and need questions to find out your client's problems and needs, work best and form a logical sequence; whereas asking a relatively large number of background questions, fewer problem, implications or need questions, and introducing solutions after the stage of asking background questions, works less well.

The reason for this difference in success rate is very simple. The first follows the customer's buying sequence, the latter makes us talk about ourselves, our company and our facilities/services which distances the approach from the customer.

Each type of question has an equivalent approach based on a statement, and the same sequence can be used as with questions, that is:

Background – problems – implications – needs, and statements can be most confidently used when we already have a thorough understanding of the client's situation. Thus, they are more often used after questioning or during more detailed meetings. For example, instead of asking 'What will these senior people expect?', you could say 'Consequently, as they are so senior, you will want to make a positive impression on them and make it a memorable experience.'

Statements should be used when the salesperson has a thorough understanding of the client's situation. They are usually used after questioning to reinforce and clarify that both the salesperson and the client have the same understanding at that given stage in the meeting.

Agreeing needs

Discovering customer needs, while it may be an important step, is not all that must be done. While knowing what the customer wants and why they want it will help, if the information is obtained in a way which makes it clear to the customer exactly what you know, this will do more. The customer must know you know, and this is important: it implies agreement of needs. What does this mean in practice? Well, that you do not just say to yourself, 'So he is interested in making a very good impression on those he books in with us.' Nor is it sufficient if you discover why, saying (to yourself) 'Because they are senior people and his customers.' On such key issues this must be re-checked. The client must be asked, 'Because of the people they are, you will want the whole experience of visiting you – and staying here – to give a first-class impression, is that right?'

If the answer is affirmative you know you are on target. It may also be more useful later to refer back to this in a way that recaps: 'You did say impact on customers was the important thing', rather than suggest, 'It seems to *me* therefore that what you want is . . .'

So, can you now move on to presenting your case, sure that everyone's needs are understood and agreed? Sorry, no; there is still more to be done before the opening stage is complete.

Establishing priorities

Clients will normally have a mix of needs and rarely will they be equally important. The next stage, as a customer's needs are established, is to identify and agree on their priority. Questions that will establish this must, therefore, be included in early stages of conversation.

As questioning reveals the needs, it may well be that conflicts become apparent: 'I want this room, with the layout tailored to our requirements and at the lowest possible quote.' All these factors may be possible, individually. But which is most important? A particular room the client knows and has used before may be available and this may meet the need reasonably well. But will it be well enough? If the buyer really wants a tailored solution, is he prepared to consider other dates? And so on and so on. There may be a neat list of three key priorities, or a complex picture of many different factors to be taken into account. In either case the principle is the same, we have to try to sort out the customer's priorities, not simply form a view of what the priorities would be for most customers (much less what we think they should be).

Again, this adds to our information base and can be of great use as the meeting progresses, guiding us towards the right presentation, one that reflects the customer's priorities.

Creating (or extending) needs
In addition, questioning will often identify hidden, unstated needs, sometimes beyond an initially stated position. For example, a simple question about a menu or seating arrangement may indicate that the final dinner of a residential meeting is special; and give a hint of additional sales opportunities (a more lavish meal, additional drinks etc.) beyond what was originally expected.

Clients with strong needs will often buy with very little encouragement. Many clients, however, are satisfied with existing arrangements. They will maintain the *status quo* unless something causes them to become dissatisfied. When we are faced with this situation we must, in fact, create some dissatisfaction before the client will consider a change. This must be done without criticizing the customer's previous decisions, which may well make him defensive. This can most readily be done by showing that due to factors outside his control, the situation is unsatisfactory. Many outside factors can be used in this way: other people's actions and attitudes; the behaviour of materials, products or systems; market forces and local, national or world events; natural phenomena like the weather, and many others.

Listening
A final point about questioning. You do not just have to ask questions, you have to listen to the answers; and what you do next should be based on those answers. If you proceed apparently as if you had not heard, and the prospect feels they are hearing the

'standard pitch', something that bears no relation to their spoken requirements, you will naturally not be so well received. In Figure 5.1 (page 91), the checklist suggests some routes to making sure you make listening an active process.

Other information

One thing that may become clear as questioning proceeds is that they are considering a competitor, or have used other venues in the past. You may well pick up useful facts about this: what costs were involved, what sort of arrangements were made – this may be worth documenting and passing on to some central point on the sales side. What you personally pick up may not be significant; together with other information from your colleagues it may paint a useful and fuller picture. Figure 5.2 (page 92) shows an example of a form designed to collect this sort of intelligence.

Conclusion

This early stage is vital; as the old saying has it: 'You get only one chance to make a good first impression.' Not only are clients making judgements on competence and approach at this stage, but the success of all that follows is dependent on the information base being established. What precisely is next will be based on this information, and is the first step towards an approach that will differentiate us from our competitors and secure the business in competitive situations.

At the end of the opening stage, what sort of view should the customer have of the salesperson? Assume that they have never met before. The initial impressions are important. The immediate view should be of someone professional; that is, being well turned-out, getting down to business positively, having an instant customer orientation, likely to know what they are talking about, being well organized and, overall, worth giving a hearing.

The opening stage should build on this first view. As it progresses, then to the above should be added a feeling that the way the salesperson is working is tailored to the customer, in other words what is being said is 100 per cent appropriate; evidence that they are appreciating, understanding and getting to grips with the customer's point of view; and also perhaps, as

1. **Want to listen** This is easy once you realize how useful it is to the sales process.

2. **Look like a good listener** If they can see they have your attention, customers will be more forthcoming.

3. **Understand** It is not just the words but what lies behind them that you must note.

4. **React** Let them see you have heard, understood and are interested. Nods, small comments, etc. will encourage.

5. **Stop talking** Other than small comments, you cannot listen and talk simultaneously. Do not interrupt.

6. **Use empathy** Put yourself in the other person's shoes and make sure you really appreciate their point of view.

7. **Check** If necessary, ask questions to clarify matters as the conversation proceeds. An understanding based, even partly, on guesses is dangerous. But ask diplomatically, do not say 'You did not explain that very well'.

8. **Remain unemotional** Too much thinking ahead 'However will I cope with that objection?' can distract.

9. **Concentrate** Allow nothing to distract you.

10. **Look at your customer** Nothing is read more rapidly as disinterest than an inadequate focus of attention.

11. **Note particularly the key points** Edit what you are told to make what you need to retain manageable.

12. **Avoid personalities** It is the ideas and information that matters, not what you think of the person; this can distract.

13. **Do not lose yourself in subsequent argument** Some thinking ahead may be necessary (you listen faster than they can talk, so it is possible); too much and you suddenly find you have missed something.

14. **Avoid negatives** To begin with at least, signs of disagreement (even visually) can make the customer clam up.

15. **Make notes** Do not trust your memory, and if it is polite to do so, ask permission.

Figure 5.1: Active listening to obtain information – checklist

Source of
information obtained ———————————— From: ——————————
(e.g. customer name)

———————————— Date: ——————————

Competitor(s) ——————————   For circulation to:

Competitor:	Details	Competitor:	Office comments

Compiled by: ————————————————————

Figure 5.2: Competitive information form

appropriate, to the kind of business that may be involved. This is very different from, and much more impressive than, their being seen simply as 'good with customers' in a general sense.

The salesperson should be seen as:

- technically competent;
- numerate;
- avoiding inappropriate jargon;
- creative;
- prepared to listen.

and, very important, the customer must feel they are interested in him, and ideally, interesting to deal with.

2. Presenting the case

There are many different things to be done during the opening stages, perhaps more than meets the eye; thereafter the second stage – presenting your case – is the core of the whole process.

It is during this stage of the sales meeting that the salesperson has to satisfy the needs and priorities of the client (already established during the opening stage) with the relevant services they offer. Again the action springs from the appropriate stage of the buying process. The client's mental demands are:

1. Will your ideas help me?
2. What are the snags?

This means that they have four objectives: to make ideas understandable, attractive and convincing (this is what we mean by *persuasive*) and to get feedback that the first three have been successfully achieved.

Each of these elements can be considered in turn and then have to be deployed together in a cohesive and effective conversation (indeed this may have to be conducted on foot as you go round the venue, something reviewed at the end of this section).

Making ideas understandable

This is the basis of all communication, and is especially important in *persuasive* communication. Now, of all the things you do in selling, the core process of telling people about your product or service is the one you no doubt feel you do best. Whatever else, people understand you. Or do they? Communication is never as straightforward as it might seem.

Misunderstandings occur all too easily and clarity must be achieved before persuasion is possible. Achieving clarity should not be taken for granted; a mistake can easily be made as you relate something you know well and deal with regularly.

Without taking due care, however, you may find someone saying 'What do you mean?' in response to something you have said. Sometimes you initiate the correction, 'But I meant . . .' and sometimes too people will say to you 'You want me to do what?' Because, as has been said, communication is not always as easy as it seems; and this shows itself in a number of ways.

It can suffer from being unclear, '. . . you fit the thing on to that sprocket thing and . . .' (just try it). Or imprecise, '. . . then it's about a mile' (three miles later . . .). It can be so full of jargon that we find ourselves saying 'manual excavation device', instead of 'spade'. Or it can be gobbledegook, 'Considerable difficulty has been encountered in the selection of optimum materials and experimental methods, but this problem is being attacked vigorously and we expect the development phase will proceed at a satisfactory rate.' ('We are looking at the handbook and trying to decide what to do.') So much so that the sense is diluted. There are innumerable barriers to communication, not least the assumptions, prejudices and inattention of those on the receiving end.

All this may simply cause a bit of confusion, and take a moment to sort out, or it can cause major problems either immediately or later. But there is never more likely to be problems than when there is an intention to get someone to do something, i.e. to buy from you. At least as many sales are probably lost simply because the customer is not clear about what – exactly what – the salesperson means, as are ever lost for any other reasons. It is an area that is worth giving some thought and consideration to. What helps to make communication clear? Three main factors affect this, they are:

Structure and sequence

Presentations should always be structured around the client's needs. For example, 'So in choosing a venue, your first concern is service, your second is visual aids, and your third is an appropriate environment for the meeting. Let's look at the service aspect first, and then deal with the others . . .'

It is also important to conclude one aspect before moving to the next, and to take matters in a logical order.

Visual aids

People understand and remember more when information is presented in visual form. Plans, pictures and brochures can also strengthen the clarity of the presentation. In using them follow the basic rules, keep them hidden until they are needed, keep quiet while they are being examined (people cannot concentrate on two things at once) and remove after use to avoid any distraction.

Note: The venue itself is, of course, a very significant visual aid and gives you much greater possibilities for utilizing the impact visualization makes than is the case in many other industries. Another visual aid which is always at your meetings is you, and how you act and appear can be used in exactly the same way. These factors come together in the 'show-round'. Comments about this appear in the appendix at the end of this chapter (page 118); you can either look at this next and return to the sequence of events reviewed here or add that element following the principles of the four main stages of the sales meeting.

Jargon

Every company and industry has its own language or jargon and the hospitality world is no exception. Some jargon can be useful, if pitched at the right level, but overall the presentation must use the client's language. This means utilizing words and terms which you are certain the client understands and avoiding words and terms which can be misinterpreted in any way, e.g. 'Our facilities are cheap', 'a provisional booking'. At the same time we have to concentrate on:

Making ideas attractive

Providing the client understands us and, as a result of a good opening, we are focusing on their needs, the key task is to show them that what you are describing will help them achieve their objectives.

The client's behaviour in decision-making – acting to satisfy a need – was referred to earlier. The stronger the need, the greater the impact of the solution, favourably or unfavourably. By a combination of questions, statements and careful listening, you have brought the customer to state his needs.

So we now have a client with needs and a salesperson with proposals. At first glance they may appear far apart. For example, consider a meeting organizer who wants to 'keep costs down'. An up-market venue may feel they face problems but, if the meeting is important, the people likewise, then the details of the facilities can be presented as meeting these people's expectations and needs, helping ensure the meeting goes well. The client would better state his needs as value for money in achieving this outcome. The venue in fact can fit logically with the requirement.

What the salesperson has done is to describe what the client will get out of the arrangement, and what the arrangement will *do* for him. Put simply, the client can see the desirable results from his point of view, of using this particular venue and all it offers.

Desirable results from the listener's point of view are called *benefits*. They are what your ideas will *do for your customers*, not what your ideas are.

People do not buy venues and facilities for what they are: they buy them for what they will do for them. (Even works of art and antiques are not bought for what they are. They are bought for the satisfaction they give their owners, whether it be visual pleasure, the satisfaction of impressing visitors, or the satisfaction of having an asset that appreciates in value faster than other forms of investment.)

Benefits provide the logical link between your client's needs and proposals. Benefits are what your client gets out of them; not what your company puts into them. Even then, one user or buyer may see them as benefit (i.e. desirable results from his point of view), while another may not see them as benefits at all. He may see them as positive disadvantages. For example, consider the following statement made by a salesman about a motorcycle, and the reactions on hearing it of a worried parent who is being pressured by his teenage son to buy it: 'This can do well over a ton without you realizing it.'

Thus it is not enough to say what your product will do. You have to select those benefits that match your listener's needs, e.g. 'Your son will find it very safe to ride.'

Similarly closer to home. Take layout in a meeting-room (something that perhaps brings us back to jargon – make sure that when you say 'U-Shape' or 'Boardroom style' the client under-stands *exactly* what you mean). Saying: 'We can arrange it in a U' is simply a factual statement. What does it mean to them? What are the benefits? For a trainer it will have to do with com-munication. A U-shape allows easy communication between trainer and participants (as does a schoolroom style layout) but also allows good communication between and amongst the participants, none of whom will have their backs to each other. This will facilitate certain kinds of discussion, though it may also make the process of control more difficult, making some people dislike it. Similar thinking can be applied to many of the aspects of discussion with clients; in each case you have to know the facts involved (in this case the way a trainer will view layout) and stress the benefits.

Types of benefit

There are three types of benefit we can use:

- Benefits to the listener in his job: 'It will ensure the meeting runs like clockwork.'
- Benefits to the listener as a person: 'They will marvel at the way it is organized.'
- Benefits to others in whom he is interested, e.g. colleagues, family, friends, and most often – participants. 'They will find it a memorable experience.'

Which are the most important? Again, the ones that fit in best with the listener's needs.

How many benefits?

When we think about what we need to say we will be able to identify many benefits that can be derived from them; but beware of using too many, believing that the more you use, the more attractive your proposals become.

The old saying, 'It is too good to be true' applies here. Too many benefits begin to stretch your listener's credulity. It is the 'match' that makes the difference here.

Increasing the effect of benefits

We can make benefits more effective by combining them in a logical sequence so that finally the listener's need is met, e.g. 'With this room you can have a layout that facilitates participation (benefit). This means people will get more from the meeting (benefit) and motivation will be high (benefit).'

Overall you make the impression you want and ensure that the meeting content is well received (benefit and satisfaction). To know what benefits to put forward, you must understand the needs of the buyer to whom you sell and the organization he presents. Firms often have more than one decision-maker, so it is essential to pinpoint your contact within the hierarchy in order to relate to them accurately (see Figure 5.3).

Thus a managing director (Decider) may ask his secretary (Influencer/Gatekeeper) to check out a short list of hotels the marketing manager (Influencer/User) wants for a product launch with his team (Users). If the marketing manager's secretary then handles the admin., there is another gatekeeper. Some circumstances give rise to much greater complexity.

Next, we need to add a further element if we are to make a genuinely persuasive case; after all we are seen as having an axe to grind, what we say prompts clients to feel 'He would say that, wouldn't he.' So, we must:

Make ideas convincing

While the customer wants to know how our recommendations

Users of service:
- may initiate;
- may specify;
- may veto.

Influencers:
- may help specify;
- may provide 'expert' objective opinion and information;
- may be outsiders;
- may be involved in setting criteria for judging between alternative suppliers.

Buyers:
- the unit that has formal authority to buy, or has an important influencing role on the decision to buy;
- may be measured on the primarily financial aspects (e.g. prices, discounts).

Deciders:
- may be the buyers;
- may be the end-users;
- are frequently the senior members of the end-user department;
- may well be the people who control the budget for the service.

Gatekeepers:
- those who control the flow of information (or lack of it) to others;
- may have the role of an influencer, a buyer or a decider.

Figure 5.3: Typical roles within the decision-making process

will help him, he also needs to know what the recommendations are, particularly if they involve any effort or cost on his part.

Similarly, he may need proof that the claims you make for your proposals, services or ideas are achievable. He needs to know, 'What are the facts?' For example, if we say, 'We can make sure the meeting goes well', the client may want to know how – not unreasonably. Of course there are exceptions to this. If your doctor says, 'This treatment will clear the infection in seven days', you will probably not want to know why or how, because you don't need proof. You implicitly accept what he says. Some salespeople build a similar level of confidence with their clients and make claims for their recommendations which are never questioned. Whilst this is a good position to aim to achieve, and there should certainly be an advisory element to selling meetings, we cannot assume that we can state benefits without ever having to substantiate them.

Therefore, we need to know in what ways claims can be upheld.

There are three ways of doing it:

* Telling the client what he has to do and how he has to do it to obtain the benefits. 'You can increase participation with this room layout.'
* Mentioning the features that produce a benefit: '. . . because it is our own equipment and our staff are familiar with it.'
* Quoting examples of what has been achieved elsewhere (third-party references): 'You'll be able to organize three syndicates that way (benefit) by using the full suite. We had a company (quote name) using just that arrangement last week (third party) and all went well.'

Let us look at the last two in more detail. First, features. These are anything connected with the venue, facilities, service and the organization behind them, including staff, policies, and so on.

For example:

Facilities	**Services**
Design	Speed
Equipment	Availability
Operation	Credit
Mobility	Pre-sales advice
Display	
Availability	
Appearance	

Companies	**People**
Time established	Knowledge
Reputation	Skill
Location	Character
Philosophy	Availability

Labour relations	Training
Size	Specialists
Policies	Numbers
Financial standing	
Organization.	

All can produce benefits.

Most people know a lot about their own organization and what it offers; but most people are by nature self-centred. The two combined can spell disaster in selling, because they often lead to the salespeople talking only features, assuming that they alone will impress the client. Occasionally the client may be impressed because he is sufficiently expert to deduce the benefits, but many clients are not experts, neither can we rely on them being bothered to make the appropriate deductions. Equally, features can produce undesirable as well as desirable results in clients' minds, e.g:

Salesman: 'And with this room there is space to serve the tea at the back.' *Client 1:* 'Oh dear, it will interrupt the meeting. *Client 2:* 'Good. That'll keep everyone together.'

The lesson is clear. Clients do not pay for features, they pay for benefits. Protect features and ensure a favourable response by telling the client why each feature is valuable to him. That's what is meant by 'product knowledge' – knowing what you sell will do as well as what it is.

Secondly, third-party references. These are other users or people who approve our ideas. They can be powerful persuaders, but are most effective if we follow four simple rules:

1. Use them to support the case, not as arguments in themselves, e.g. 'For example . . .', not: 'You ought to do what Acme Engineering are doing . . .'
2. When mentioning names, make sure they are people or organizations that the client respects, e.g. 'John thinks it's a good idea.' 'In that case, I'll support it.'
3. Choose third parties whose circumstances are similar to those facing this customer, e.g. 'Archibold's Engineering who are about your size and similarly organized . . .'

4. Don't simply mention the third party. Tell your listener the benefits that the third party obtained, e.g. 'For example, Acme Engineering have found that by using this arrangement, they have been able to reduce their training budget and yet hold meetings somewhere everyone likes.'

Ensuring that a case includes sufficient credibility is crucial. It can be a particular fault of the most impressive property to assume that it speaks for itself. To an extent it may do so, but the job is to get the client envisaging how the use of the property would work and the particulars of this need reinforcing. One small addition to what is done – laying out a row of chairs to make it absolutely clear that the capacity is as you say, for instance – can make all the difference.

Beating the competition
It is very rare that we are in a monopoly position. In most cases we will be in competition with other companies, other people, or even with the client's own views on what should be done. We can reduce the impact of competition by combining benefits and features in a number of ways:

1. *Simple benefit statement*
   'You will encourage participation with this layout.'
2. *Comparison statement*
   Here compare the benefits of the recommendations with the disadvantages of a competitive recommendation, e.g. 'You will encourage participation with this layout, whereas schoolroom style has people with their backs to each other.'
3. *Sandwich statement*
   In this method your ideas and their benefits are the first and last things the client hears, e.g. 'You will encourage participation with this layout; in addition, this room means you can serve coffee in the alcove and save the cost of a second room.'

Many words have both literal meaning and connotations. Make sure the client interprets words in the same way that they are meant.

All this assumes we are doing most of the talking at this stage. This may be so. But we should not be doing it all, we need to involve the client and we need to know how to check what the customer is thinking. Hence:

Obtaining feedback
Obtaining and using feedback can modify the content, method, and pace of our selling. The two methods for obtaining feedback are simple and effective:

1. Observation
Use eyes and ears to determine his reaction to proposals. Is he using words, expressions and actions which indicate interest and understanding? E.g.:
> 'That sounds interesting.'
> 'Really?'
> 'I see.'
> 'Let me make a note of that.'

Is he watching you or gazing out of the window?
Are his fingers tapping impatiently on his desk?
Is he beginning to look through his other papers or glancing at the clock?
Is he leaning forward, obviously paying attention?

Watch and listen. If no verbal response is forthcoming and the client's body language is unclear, stop talking and wait for a comment.

2. Questions
If we get neither verbal nor other forms of feedback, we can use a range of questions to elicit specific responses, e.g.:
a) To test understanding: 'Have I made it clear how the layout will be?'
b) To check his appreciation of benefits: 'Do you see how this layout will make the participation easier to control?'
c) To check his reaction to a feature: 'What do you think of this layout?'
d) To check that you're still discussing his needs: 'Is the cost reduction what you're mainly concerned about?'

The response to these questions will tell us where we are in the buying sequence and guide us accordingly. By asking them we will also keep him involved in the discussion and prevent problems later on.

At this stage we should be well on the way to a successful sale. In the opening stage we identified, explored, and agreed on the client's needs. Then, in the sales presentation we put forward solutions in an attractive, convincing and understandable way.

Note: Remember much of the foregoing takes place 'on the move' as you show people the property – see 'show-round' appendix at the end of the chapter (page 118).

Contractual arrangements

You need to remember that what you sell is a contractual arrangement. Customers may not realize it (or choose to ignore it) but the arrangement made between you and them involves contractual issues. This aspect must be dealt with carefully; salespeople are sometimes wary of introducing topics that may make the overall deal appear less attractive to the customer, yet later customers may feel that such issues have been disguised or avoided. This is most apparent perhaps with cancellation terms, and especially so for large amounts of business, a bulk-booking of rooms, for example, or a conference or banqueting arrangement.

The terms and conditions are there to protect your company's financial position and profitability; at the same time it is important that:

- they are communicated clearly and prevent misunderstandings;
- they project efficiency and enhance the customer relationship;
- they encourage conversation of business effectively and promptly;
- they link to any other necessary arrangements and documentation.

In discussing terms and conditions, never apologize for their necessity; stress the mutual advantages, talk about working together and if necessary use a checklist to ensure you deal with everything systematically. Specifically you may want to evolve a step-by-step way of introducing, describing and making terms and conditions stick. The following illustrates the kind of progression involved:

1. Introduce the concept of contractual arrangements
This is usually better done early rather than later, though, of course, details may be left over. It is important to make it clear that contract means something confirmed in writing. Remember the moment passes; it may get progressively more difficult to introduce contractual matters later once it has been left for too long. Do not wait for the client to raise the issue; they are unlikely to do so – and link mention of the contract to the written offer.

2. Make the developing detail clear
You must be careful to spell out accurately the detail, and should not assume the client is familiar with everything – even if they have dealt with you previously. For example, do not just say 'I will reserve it provisionally', spell out what it means '. . . we will hold it for a month, and if I get other enquiries for that time . . .' (such phraseology must be precise; you may not want the client to have first option too long – if a better booking comes in during such a time you may want to force a decision).

3. Stress particularly figures and timing
There must be no misunderstanding about the details which, in the worst scenario, can cause the greatest problem. For example, are costs inclusive of tax? When is 'in a month's time' exactly? (four weeks or . . . ?). Two factors are of particular importance:

- deposit policy/timing;
- credit arrangements.

4. Check understanding
This may be as simple as an occasional 'Is that clear?', but is very important. It is no good, at a later stage, believing everything was clear and agreed between you – you need to know.

5. Document your side of arrangements

Tell clients what you will do, and follow it up efficiently and promptly in a way that sets the pattern for clear to-and-fro written confirmation. And make it easy for the client. Administrative chores breed delay, clients may prefer you to summarize details of a discussion so that they can write a couple of lines that say 'That's right'. The reverse will take longer. This may usefully be checklist-led; in other words the details that need to be documented come off an agreed internal checklist document which acts as a prompt and reminder; it can be all too easy to overlook apparently small details.

6. Ask for their confirmation

Whatever it is you want, written confirmation, a signed contract (the agreed internal-policy specifics) you need to ask – specifically – for it. It is not necessary to go round the houses; you do not need to make an issue of it (the client does, after all, see it as a business arrangement and will not be surprised), but you do need to make the process, and implications clear, and get it under way.

7. Record the action

Keep a clear note of what you have done, how the client has responded and – the most important – when it needs checking and when further action needs taking. This should clearly link to follow-up diary systems or be, infallibly, a part of the more sophisticated computer database and 'prompt' systems so many venues use today for their client records and bookings information.

8. Chase for action

This is crucial. If the client ignores key stages – and some will – we must actively remind them of their commitment. Do not feel awkward about doing this; after all, we should be following up agreed commitments ('When will you let me have the contract back?', 'By the end of the week') so clients will expect it; and besides, the penalty for delay can be very damaging. Such chasing must therefore always be systematic, courteous, but insistent.

9. Adopt the appropriate manner
Throughout the process make it clear that this is not a negative procedure; indeed ultimately it can be presented as a protection for clients (who do not wish to be left without space and facilities for an event, any more than you want to be left with gaps not utilized). So deal with it in a way that is efficient, and implies good service, that is professional; and position yourself as an appropriate point of contact from the client's viewpoint.

10. Link to follow-up
The contractual arrangement links to both the event itself and its aftermath. The supplier must deliver 'on the day'; this is their part of the contract and all the service issues are important here. Further, we should see the process described as linking to:

- *Invoicing:* and here it is most important that the invoice *accurately* reflects the agreed detail (and clients seem to find so often this is not the case), and is straightforwardly and clearly presented. This may be submitted with a personalized covering note which links to obtaining feedback about the event, the future relationship; or both. Sending the invoice, of course, implies chasing to get it paid. Again not an easy – or palpable – task, but it must be done and it is frankly easier to follow up in a way that gets it seen as a routine, rather than only when so much time has gone by that the approach must be heavy. This is vital. So is cash-flow; and these days the need to chase is, perhaps regrettably, the norm.
- *Selling-on:* as future contact is made, as a relationship is forged we want the contractual side to become easier. Next time the procedure is 'as before', and if it all went well this will be seen by the client as reasonable, straightforward and hassle-free.

When things go wrong
The approach advocated above may well help minimize the likelihood of frivolous or ill-considered change or cancellation – not a bad subsidiary objective, in fact. But sometimes, the worst will happen, and then those circumstances must be coped with.

In such a situation, a total cancellation, say, there are three broad options for action:

- *apply the 'letter of the law'*: this may be ideal and may either prevent cancellation (a reminder of the terms prompts a rethink), or secure the best deal for us financially. Sometimes this can be approached as if routine and will not be questioned. Alternatively, we are faced with the second option:
- *negotiate a compromise*: the setting of individual, exceptional terms and conditions may be necessary, certainly, if it is a better alternative to legal action or falling out with the client for the future, it may be a reasonable route, once a problem occurs.

  Note: negotiation is a skill, and a different one from communication and from selling; it is one which should not be underestimated in its complexity. As the process is important and inherent to the topic of this book, but somewhat beyond its brief, you may want to investigate this further. (My book *Conducting Successful Negotiations* (How to Books) has a section that deals specifically with negotiation techniques.)
- *make an exception*: one outcome of negotiation is that it arrives at a compromise you may regard as making a real gesture to the client, and to client goodwill. As it is always easier to sell to existing clients than find new ones, maintaining goodwill is important. Just be careful you do not end up with every case being special, and thus an exception. It can be costly and precedents are more easily set than not.

3. Handling objections

This stage is less neat. Objections can occur throughout the whole process, though perhaps most come towards the end of the presentational stage. Some objections are inevitable, a part of the weighing-up process buyers go through in which they search for the plus and the minus points of any proposition put to them. In this sense objections can be a sign of interest.

But there are other more down-to-earth reasons why objections arise that are within a salesperson's control:

- You may not have identified and agreed the customer's needs;
- You may have offered a solution too soon;
- You may have talked features instead of benefits;
- Your benefits may have been too general or too numerous;
- You may have failed to obtain or recognize feedback.

Thus, it has to be said that many objections are not inherent in customers; they are caused by salespeople. You should reduce the frequency and intensity of objections by selling well, but from time to time they will still arise.

How to keep control

The first thing to recognize is that most objections have both an emotional and rational content. Emotionally, the client becomes defensive or aggressive! Rationally, they require a logical answer to the particular objection that they have raised. To handle them successfully you will need to tackle the emotional and rational aspects separately and sequentially.

This section explains how to handle the emotional aspect and keep things under control. Its importance can be illustrated by the frequency with which current affairs programmes on radio and TV degenerate into slanging matches. If you watch them closely you will see that the trouble starts when one participant says something with which another disagrees. Instead of controlling their emotions and dealing with the point clearly and logically, they criticize each other. The rest you know only too well.

Keeping control is easier if we put ourselves in a client's position when they find disadvantages in a proposition. If we were clients, we would want the salesperson to listen to our point of view, to consider it, and to acknowledge that our point was reasonable – all before she answers. We can do the same with objections raised, keep control, and as a result allow them to consider the answer calmly and rationally.

In conversation it goes like this: Client identifies a 'snag' and voices her objections: 'I think the sound system will be too complicated for the speaker and, therefore, he won't use it.' The salesperson listens; pauses; and acknowledges: 'It probably does look complicated to anyone who hasn't seen it before and we obviously need to take that into account when we brief him.' Notice that the salesperson has not yet answered the objection. All he has done is shown understanding of the customer's point of view and met the first point in the buying sequence: 'I am important and want to be respected.' Then a more detailed answer can follow.

So often, rational answers to objections are less than successful because the client is emotionally unable to evaluate them fairly. By listening, pausing and acknowledging, we keep emotions under control and give our answers the best chance of being accepted.

Such holding remarks, as in the example just given, may be quite brief – 'That's a good point, we will certainly need to consider that' – but, despite this, they may serve another purpose. Human design is such that in the time it takes us to say a phrase such as 'We will certainly need to consider that,' there can be a considerable amount of thinking going on. Such remarks give us a chance to consider what we ought to say next. They can be invaluable if the objection has really thrown you (never let it show on your face or in your manner, incidentally), and useful much of the time when a moment's thought is valuable.

Before considering how to answer objections, we must point out that you need to understand exactly what the objection means. Never be afraid to answer a question with a question. Alternatively, if the objection comes as a challenge (without a question mark at the end), it may help to turn the objection into a question, and so establish the customer's need behind their resistance. Why are they asking this? Is it an excuse? Delaying tactics? Perhaps they have a point? An apparently straightforward comment such as 'It is very expensive' may mean a wide range of different things from 'It is more than I expected' to 'No', from 'It is more than I can agree' (though someone else might) to 'It is more than the budget' and so on. For example, on a recent course, participants who were asked to think about alternative meanings for the phrase 'It is very expensive' produced 36 meanings within ten minutes or so, most necessitating a different answer from each other.

Checking the status of the objection does not mean that you do not have to answer it. You do. Think of objections as minus signs, of different sizes, sitting on the balance the customer is conjuring up in her mind. There are only three ways of dealing with them. Either you explain that the point is not valid, and the balance is therefore more positive, as the point is removed from the minus side; or you persuade her it is less significant than she fears, so most of its weight goes; or you agree (there is no merit in trying to convince her that black is white). In all three cases, particularly the latter, the salesperson's response may need to include some re-emphasis on the positive side also. There may even be a fourth way, to actually turn what a customer describes as a minus into something positive.

You have to know your property and everything about it really well to produce good answers. The following approaches will help:

The boomerang
This approach (also useful on the telephone when aiming to fix appointments) pushes the question back to the customer:

C   I am sure I could get something less costly.
S   There are plenty around that are less expensive, it's true. However, you were saying that the level of people you aim to book in are senior managers. The impression of your company given by their staying here . . .

Pre-empting
Here the objection is assumed, avoided and dealt with.

S   You may well feel this only applies to organizations larger than yours. I would like to show you, however, how it has particular benefits for your kind of firm . . .

Delay
This is as close as you can get to not answering. In fact, you answer later.

C Now, before we get into the detail, I am concerned about the menu suggestions you submitted. They are very costly, is there an alternative?

S Yes, of course, and we need to review that. It might help if first, I understand more about the people involved, are they . . .

This is often acceptable; and customers like it if you remember to pick up a point sidelined in this way later. Make a note – do not forget.

Tacit denial

This leaves the point on one side, and concentrates on balancing factors.

C It is very expensive to use that arrangement.

S Well, it isn't the least expensive way, but it achieves the numbers and timings you wanted, which is crucial.

And on to the next point.

Final objections

Here, whatever the query, it is investigated thus:

S Apart from menus, is there anything else you need to be satisfied about before placing a booking?

The customer can then say that everything else is fine, or produce a list to be dealt with. The former remark is particularly useful near to the end of the meeting as a lead into the close.

There is a need to deal promptly and definitely (not glibly) with objections; you have to have the courage of your convictions, and sometimes a simple, but sound answer to seemingly dramatic objections that meets the point head on. A price objection, 'That's very expensive', met simply with, 'Yes, it is a considerable investment', may be followed by a long pause, after which the prospect moves on to something else. Over-reacting to comments about price, especially before you have really checked out what they mean, can lead to digging the hole deeper – at worst, spiralling into a negotiation for which there was no need and reducing profitability as you do so.

Sign	The words you should use to emphasize what the price will mean
+ (benefits)	add; added-value; in addition; plus; augment; reinforce; enhance; strengthen; develop.
− (losses)	less; reduce; minimize; contraction; condense; restrict; exclude.
x (productivity)	multiply; considerable; numerous; ample; productivity; performance; majority.
÷ (product cost)	share; divide; proportion; amortize; part; distribute; measure.
= (totality of package)	equal; equivalent; will mean; will produce; total; ultimately; outcome; benefit; results.

Figure 5.4: Dealing with price objections: some prompts

As a final illustration, we will stay with price objections. Any mechanism which prompts the right response – to any objection in fact – is useful. With price, as Figure 5.4 shows, using the mathematical symbols as a prompt to memory leads into some good responses; the words in the figure illustrate how.

So, to summarize:

- anticipate likely objections;
- select and deal with appropriate ones before they are raised;
- be seen to respond in a considered manner;
- do not be – or a least appear to be – caught out.

You should rarely be caught out by objections you have not foreseen, at least in general terms. Thus, handling them effectively is another result of good preparation. There will always be some, however, that demand you are 'quick on your feet'. An apparently unexpected objection, well-handled, can be impressive, and taken as a display of competence.

Objection handling is as much about prevention as cure; whatever route is taken, care and consideration can preserve the balance of advantages that are perceived by the customer.

4. Closing

Closing is not really a stage. It is a question and a prompt to customer commitment and action. The first rule about closing is simple: do it. It is all too easy for closings to be avoided, and with it, of course, the trauma of 'Will he say "No"?' But a close that is no more than, say, 'Does that tell you all you need at the moment?' – getting a pleasant response like 'Yes, thank you so much for all your help', followed by 'Goodbye' is not really worthy of the term 'close'. Yet it is all too easy to do no more than this; indeed it may seem appropriate at the end of a 'show-round' that seems to have gone well.

Note, however, that closing does not only apply to getting the order. We want commitments at many stages, especially in complex sales situations. The prospect may agree to:

- a meeting;
- a 'show-round';
- receive plans/literature;
- attend an exhibition;
- another meeting (or formal presentation);
- a written proposal or quotation.

All these, and more – sometimes in a sequence – are steps on the way to the sale and need the commitment gained just as much as with the order at the end of the day.

Obtaining commitment

Knowing that the objective of all selling is to obtain customer commitments often obscures the need to remember how buyers arrive at the point of commitment. They only willingly take buying decisions after they have recognized and felt needs, and are convinced that their needs will be satisfied by implementing the proposal. Thus, the best chance of success lies in doing a good job before they reach the stage of asking themselves 'What shall I do?'

Attempts to get commitment (closing) without first having created desire for the proposition will normally be seen by the customer as pressure tactics. The bigger the decision, the greater the pressure, and the stronger will be the resistance.

Closing does not cause orders, it merely converts a high desire into orders and low desire into refusals. Even when the desire is high, however, the customer may not volunteer a positive commitment. Similarly, the customer may want to make a commitment, but there are several variations of it, and the salesperson wants one particular kind. It is in these situations that closing skills are valuable; such skills concentrate the buyer's mind on the advantage to be gained from the buying decision itself.

There are certain behaviours, questions and comments indicating a general willingness to buy that can provide 'buying signals', indicating the best moment at which to close. Some of these involve:

- Tone of voice, posture, hesitation, nodding.
- Questions on details showing acceptance in principle.
- Comments expressing positive interest, attraction, etc.

These can be converted into closes, as long as you are careful not to oversell when the customer wants to make a commitment.

So, whether closing is successful or not is dependent on two things. First, there is everything you have done to date. If the preceding stages have not succeeded in stimulating sufficient interest, or if there are still objections niggling at the interest, then there is little likelihood of closing securing final agreement.

Secondly, the closing question must be put in an appropriate and positive fashion. Thus, although this is the crunch point and can sometimes be avoided because of the unpleasant possibility of getting a 'No', the commitment must actually be asked for; the only question is exactly how it is put. There are various methods. Here are some examples.

Direct request
For example, 'Shall we go ahead then and make a booking to ensure you get the date set?'

Command
'Let me have something in writing, and we will hold it provisionally.'

Immediate gain
'If you can give me the go-ahead now, I can make sure that you get priority.'

Alternatives
'We can put you in room A or B. Which would suit you better?'

Third-party reference
'You can get the advantages that Johnson's are enjoying simply by adopting the same solution. So let's put the wheels in motion.'

Question or objection
Client: 'Can the room be arranged to suit our particular requirements?'
Salesperson: 'Yes it can. How would you like us to do it?'

Best solution or summary
'The way to make this go well is to lay it out U-shape, and use two other rooms linked to the main area. Rooms A, B and C can be arranged just that way – when can we make it a firm booking?'

Assumption
'Fine, I've now got all the information I need to meet your requirements. As soon as I get back to the office I'll prepare the necessary paperwork and you'll have our specific suggestions in a day or two.'

Successful salespeople only close when they are sure that the client has been satisfied on all the key stages of the buying process.

If your first attempt to close is unsuccessful, find out why, deal with the points that arise and close again. The answer at this point may well be 'Yes'.

No matter how well a presentation is given and questions handled in selling, the prospect may still sometimes have objections to making a decision. Sometimes these are stated, but often they are reserved and come in the form 'I'll think about it'.

When this happens, simple closes may only irritate the prospect and the way forward may be unclear. Yet it is a key stage to get over, and this can be done by listing the objections: 'I agree you should think about it. However, it's possibly your experience also that when someone says they want to think about it it's because they are still uncertain about some points. In order to help our thinking on these, let's note them down.' Then make a list with room for more objections than he has; do not write any down until each is understood, and do not answer any – yet. Flush them all out and be sure there are not more to come. This enables an additional closing technique to be used: 'If I'm able to answer each of these points to your complete satisfaction, can we agree we're in business?' This is the *conditional* close. Each point listed is answered in turn, crossed off the list, and the prospect's agreement with each checked, then the close is not repeated, but assumption used to conclude matters: 'Fine, now we're in business.'

After a successful close
The job has not finished simply because the client has said 'Yes'. He may well need reassurance that he has done the right thing, so:

- thank him;
- confirm that he has made a wise decision, by stressing the benefits;
- leave or end the meeting promptly.

And see to any necessary documentation or confirmation promptly (it is useful and appreciated to tell people exactly what will be done and when).

Conclusion

Good selling often makes formal closing unnecessary. Make customers thirsty and you won't have to force them to drink. Successful salespeople only close when they are sure that the client has been satisfied on the other stages in the buying process.

If a close is needed to convert desire into action, make it attractive by emphasizing the need satisfaction that a commitment will bring.

If your first attempt to close is unsuccessful, find out why, deal with the points that arise, and close again.

Long term

Remember finally that a successful sale should start a relationship – and managing that effectively gives us a reordering client; for many the major percentage of their business comes from this category. They have to be managed professionally and we must always seek opportunities to sell on (the repeats), sell up (larger orders/broader take-up of the range we offer), and sell across (find new contacts from the first – branches, subsidiaries, etc). Next, we return to the 'show-round'.

Appendix to Chapter 5

The 'show-round'

Untold hours must be spent by hotel salespeople the world over in showing prospective customers around their particular property. Because it takes time – for a large venue such as a major conference centre it could be an hour or more – and because it is so crucial to the prospective buyer (there are many who will never commit without seeing what they are booking), it is an area of considerable opportunity. As such it must be done well or considerable waste of time and potential business will be involved.

And is it done well? In my experience, and that of others I consulted before writing this, the answer is often negative. Often this is because of the 'automatic pilot' syndrome which I have mentioned before. It is done unthinkingly, in the way it has always been done, and suffers as a result from being seen as the 'general tour'; and indeed it is. Everyone goes the same route and receives the same patter, something that is inclined to be perpetuated – passed on from one to another in a way which, if it is unthinking, can end up as the blind leading the blind.

The show-round is a process which must be used to maximize the growing positive impression being made on each and every prospect. It is a vital part of the sales process. Venue facilities are certainly visual, maybe dramatically so – but they do *not* sell themselves. Showing people around is only part of the job; it is *how* they are shown around that will make the difference.

The key is inherent in one important fact. Potential clients are not interested in 'having a look to see whether it is nice'; *they want to see, to imagine how their event would work in a particular venue.* The job is to help them to do just that.

It follows that there should be no such thing as the 'standard tour'. Each inspection visit must be tailored for the particular prospect in question, and must reflect their needs. So, always consider individually:

- who they are;
- what you know of their needs (and their organization);
- how used are they likely to be to 'checking somewhere out';
- what is their likely role in any future event;

and arrange, and conduct, things accordingly. This calls on knowledge of the prospect built up at an earlier stage, and this base of information will no doubt be filled out as you proceed.

Before the event
- think about the sequence in which you go around the facilities (one way is chronologically following the possible future event, stating where delegates arrive, check in and so on);

- think about who you need to brief (reception to expect them, the restaurant manager, etc.);
- think about what you need to check (are areas you want to visit clean, accessible and unlocked?);
- think about what you need to arrange (layouts, visual aids, etc.) – think about what you need with you (brochures, photos, room plans, etc.).

During the tour
- explain (and agree) what you plan to do;
- allow time for the visual impact to sink in (no talking);
- put them into a position of experiencing how it will be, rather than simply looking at it (e.g. get a speaker up on the platform);
- ask as many questions as you give out facts and get their feedback.

After the tour
- summarize the (agreed) appropriateness;
- allow final questions;
- fill in final detail;
- link to administrative action (e.g. confirmation of any detail).

However, it would be naïve to assume that the sale will now fall into our lap, because the client will, as part of the buying sequence, automatically consider possible disadvantages in the proposal. The 'show-round' is an integral part of the whole meeting which should flow seamlessly from meeting-style discussion to tour and back again. It needs planning, and that plan must relate to:

- the individual client;
- what you know about them, their general attitudes and their specific need;
- when you are to show them round;
- what you will find on the way (from people to redecorating in process);

and should utilize and make the best of all the good things you have to show *provided they are appropriate*. Remember, people do not always want to see every nook and cranny of the place. Some things may be positioned as options: '. . . and would you find it useful to see . . . as we are going through to the . . .' The point made earlier to the effect that the process is better described as a demonstration, something to give them the feel of the place as *if they were using it* is the best way to focus your mind on what to do and how to go about it.

Consider the differences evidenced in the following scenario:

A conference organizer is looking around a hotel. He stands just inside the door of the room suggested for his planned event. The room is empty (or, sometimes, contains the last, messy, remnants of what went on there the previous day), and the salesperson points out the features. He lists the individually controllable lights, the good acoustics, the easy way in which equipment can be brought in and set up and so on. Alternatively, the conference buyer is taken right into the room. He is not told about the acoustics, they are demonstrated as the sales person speaks to him from the far end of the room, he is offered the opportunity to try out his slides, he is taken to stand on the verandah where the morning break can be taken. Such an experience lets the person 'live' *their* event, imagine it happening – successfully – in that hotel, that room. It is not, or should not be, the standard tour, but is tailored to the person instead. An organizing secretary will be made especially familiar with the reception area, and aspects of the meeting with which they will be involved.

A conference speaker will be encouraged to see how they feel on the platform or at the front. If the room can be laid out, even in part, as it will be on the day, so much the better (yes, I know it takes time and trouble, but so does finding another prospect when one says no). In this way the prospect literally begins to take part in the selling process, and can leave the demonstration able to say 'I *know* it will work here.'

The form in Figure 5.5, or a tailored version of it, may well help you think through the best approach either generally or for an individual client.

Mix letting some things speak for themselves (I do not need repeatedly telling what a lovely view there is from the patio, I would rather have a moment's silence to appreciate it) with powerful description and getting the person involved, and you will make the show-round add a real 'edge' to your sales approach and bring out the best of any venue.

What to show (or not)	**Route** _____ → _____ → _____ → _____ → _____ → _____ → _____ → _____ → _____ →

How	**Dangers**	**Opportunities**
_____	_____	_____
_____	_____	_____
_____	_____	_____
_____	_____	_____
_____	_____	_____
_____	_____	_____
_____	_____	_____

CHECK:

Before: _____

_____

_____

During: _____

_____

_____

After: _____

_____

_____

Figure 5.5: Show-round planning sheet

6 Client management: securing and developing existing customers

ONE OF the signs once posted around an American retail store as a reminder to staff read: 'WARNING – Customers are perishable!' Quite right, practically nothing is more important to any business than existing or regular customers. They are the life-blood of the business and for many produce a significant percentage of the business. In one company they have a series of follow-up systems they call the LYBUNT system. It stands for 'Last Year But Unfortunately Not This', and is designed to stop anyone falling into this category.

It is a sobering event if, when you telephone someone you have not spoken to for a while, you find they have just made a booking with someone else. Typically the reaction is to say something like: 'Why ever didn't you let us quote?', but if the response to this is: 'We didn't seem to have heard from you for a while', it is difficult to do other than accept the blame.

Customer relationships are fragile: 'Out of sight is out of mind' as the old saying has it: A customer's business with you is important to you; they, however, may see you as 'just another supplier'. Fixing hotel arrangements may be seen as a chore and you will simply not remain, automatically, at the top of their mind, even if a first experience of the hotel proved to be exactly what they wanted – satisfaction is not a guarantee of repeat bookings. And they are vulnerable; leave them alone too long and they will be prey to your competitors. Such relationships need nurturing. The message of this chapter is so simple it can be summed up in three words: *Keep in touch*.

But it is not as easy to practise as it is to state. Other pressures interfere with your best intentions, and there may also be a difficulty in thinking what on earth to say in what you may see as 'yet another follow-up'. Yet the potential rewards are very considerable. While the principle is simply stated above, there is more to it to be borne in mind if you are to pursue things systematically and certainly.

One of the best salesmen I have ever encountered was in the hotel business. I met him on an overseas trip in Thailand. I was setting up a series of management workshops for an organization in Bangkok and the client wanted them to run outside of the city. So one Friday I found myself sitting in a coach travelling to Pattaya, which in the days this occurred was a newish and well-regarded resort area. I got chatting to the man sitting next to me who turned out to be working for another hotel in the resort, not the one I was booked in to visit. In the hour that remained of our journey he not only discovered what I was doing, he persuaded me to spend the weekend at his hotel and check that out instead. He ignored all my protests that I was booked in elsewhere and said he would phone and cancel for me (and he did!). I spent the weekend there; the hotel was excellent and the meetings were duly run there six or eight weeks later.

He kept in touch regularly thereafter and now some 18 years later I still hear from him every six months or so. He has moved hotel, hotel group, and country more than once. Yet never has his follow-up system faltered. As a result he has received additional business over the years and recommendations too – all for the price of a few stamps. Follow-up is an attitude and a habit, but what makes it work and where does the process start?

It starts on the day you identify a new contact. And it goes on until you take a conscious decision to stop maintaining contact. You may well need as a starting-point some kind of enquiry form. Such a form, perhaps one you design (or adapt) bestows the proper importance on the enquiry. It should act first as a checklist: to prompt whoever is taking the enquiry to ask the right questions and obtain, so far as possible, the right information. Small things make a difference. A job title may tell you something about the likely decision-making power of an enquirer (though it is not, of course, an infallible guide); a note of the source of the enquiry may help identify which promotional or prospecting methods are working best.

Secondly, it can act as a prompt and can be used to ensure that an enquiry is progressed promptly and efficiently, and followed up, specifying and recording action. A form can be made to perform this role well if the last entry in terms of what is happening is always a note of what you plan to do *next*. This acts as a reminder and can link to a diary or follow-up system. It may not always be possible to complete such a form totally; for example, the prospect may not wish to tell you (or may not know) how he came across your name, but anything beyond the basic information may help; that is it may increase the chances that you can deal with it in a way that ensures a sale results.

Thirdly, such a form builds up a record. This is not its prime purpose – ensuring action is more important – but the record is necessary. Thinking of it as a record system may end up making the system less effective – the danger is that it is felt it is *just* for the record and neglected as a result.

This starting-point does not only respond to an enquiry; there is no reason why anything that then needs progressing through cannot use the same system, so a successful prospect call for instance gives rise to the same information and the form follows the progress of the lead it becomes. It may be best on A4-size paper (the same size as company letterhead). In some companies enquiry documentation is on coloured paper to make them stand out visibly in the office, or they may need to be on carbonless sets to facilitate copying to others in the organization, and these days they may very well be linked to a computerized customer record system and most usually looked at and used 'on-screen'. However it is done, it must be tailored to your company and the way you work to ensure the right action takes place at the right time and in the right way.

An example of such a form is shown in Figure 6.1. You may have, and use, something similar; if not, this may provide a basis for adaptation (it is not suggested you follow this slavishly).

To: _____ Date: _____

From: _____ Reference number: _____

Name of prospect company: _____

Address: _____

Contact name/position: _____ Phone: _____

Subsidiary/division of: _____

Nature of business: _____

Size of organization: _____

Source of lead: cold call _____

referral _____

promotion_____

other _____

Comments on any past contact: _____

Indicated business opportunity:_____

_____

Action requested: _____

_____

By, time:_____

Record of actions taken:

Date	Action

Sales lead actioned by: _____

Date: _____

Copies to: _____

Figure 6.1: Sales action required

Persistence pays off

Without a doubt this is true. There is a host of reasons, even once interest has been expressed or an enquiry lodged, for clients to do nothing. You want the business and want a decision as soon as possible; they want to get on with other things and regard the whole thing as a distraction. When you follow up and someone says they are 'away', 'in a meeting' or 'busy and will get back to you', it is very easy to become paranoid and feel that interest is dying.

But they may just be away, on holiday, in a meeting or busy with something of greater priority to them than finalizing an arrangement with you. They may still be interested – in their own good time. So, do not be tempted to give up: keep the contacts going. When they are ready to do something more about it, you want to be at the forefront of their mind.

Remember too that lead times can be long. I was interrupted in writing some of this chapter by a telephone call from a venue to finalize arrangements for a short sales course, and when I got out the file I noticed it was almost a exactly a year since the conversation began. The time taken by linking actions in this case was minimal, but important. Sometimes you will find things take even longer than this and yet are still worthwhile.

Ring the changes as you persist. Write (or fax) as well as telephone them, and try to make any written, and therefore less transient, contacts other than routine, which so often comes over as simply saying: 'Do I get any business yet?'. For example, after a series of abortive contacts with a publisher about the interest they had expressed in the possibility of my doing some (more) writing for them, I sent a sheet of letterhead on which was simply one boxed paragraph. It read:

Struggling author, patient, reliable (non-smoker), seeks commissions on business topics. Novel formats preferred, but anything considered within reason. Ideally 100 or so pages on a topic like sales excellence sounds good; maybe with some illustrations. Delivery of the right quantity of words – on time – guaranteed. Contact me at the above address or telephone number, or meet on neutral ground carrying a copy of *Publishing News* and wearing a carnation.

The confirmation arrived, by fax, the following day! And I remember thinking for a moment – 'Can I send that?' - but it was clearly not inappropriate (you can now read the result: *The Sales Excellence Pocketbook* – Management Pocketbooks).

Finally, of course, you have to cut your losses. Not all acorns grow into giant oak trees and not all leads produce business, but deciding to pursue them no longer should be a considered decision and even then there may be another action that takes over – putting them on a general mailing list perhaps.

Once they say 'Yes'

Every customer should be regarded as potentially a source of repeat business. Action to make that eventuality more likely should start as soon as they say 'Yes' to any current arrangement. Their thinking about whether they will return begins at this point; later, when they look back as they consider something else, a variety of things may come to mind. So consider:

- confirmations of an existing arrangement should be clear and efficient;
- any handover to operational staff should be nicely handled;
- you may need to keep in touch and see them 'on the day'; you cannot do this with everyone and everything, of course, but do think about which are worth the time;
- how things finish up and the immediate follow-up.

It is worth a slight digression to mention two points here:

- checkout of a hotel is often one of the least impressive moments in terms of efficiency and convenience for the customer. Often it is time-consuming, often there are details that seem incorrect ('But I haven't touched the minibar'), and rarely is anything said or given to act as a reminder or prompt to future booking – a card, a name, even small touches add to the one mandatory take-away, the account; and this is often the least attractive sort of computer printout.

- soon after the departure may be a good moment for some follow-up action. Some hotels telephone conference/meeting users in the next day or two. Fine: as a client myself I find this pleasant enough if it is nicely done; but do not say 'Was everything all right?'; apart from being somewhat banal, they will certainly feel you should *know* the arrangements went well. Better to ask about the way their meeting went, rather than about the physical arrangements.

The key here is to link forward to the future and the additional sales possibilities that may exist there. Numbers of things may be relevant at this stage: from a questionnaire sent to check service standards to just a 'Thank you' note for the business. Whatever is done – and what it is may vary customer by customer as appropriate – it should then be regarded as the first communication in a series of communications to keep in touch.

Ongoing communication

Again the key thing here is that, whether action is taken, what that action is and how often it is instigated are considered. There will be some customers who warrant no follow-up action: a single overseas visitor, perhaps, who says he will not return. But many need to be contacted, and recontacted.

Some of this contact will be corporate. A hotel or group will maintain a mailing list and send a range of things of a standard nature to people, i.e. the same thing to all those on the list (or a segment of it). Sometimes this kind of mailing may include a personally addressed letter – no doubt computer-generated – but it is essentially a standard shot. Some contacts warrant no more action than this.

At the other end of the scale is the major corporate user who will agree to meet with you regularly, indeed expects to do so, and who also expects other forms of contact as well. In between are the majority of contacts for whom you must decide a frequency of contact, some of which may take the form of personal meetings; and some other forms. Some kind of systematic approach may help here. Many companies divide their contact lists into categories: A – B – C – D, with each category receiving a set amount and mix of contact, at least while they remain in the particular category. Most salespeople will have a number of contacts who, at any particular moment, demand an individual approach. With these you have to consider:

* frequency of contact;
* methods of contact;
* reasons for contact;

each of which is worth a word in turn.

Frequency of contact

The rule here is simple: contact should be sufficiently often, and regular, to ensure recall and do the job of developing the business, and no more. Just going for more and more frequent contact may become self-defeating – customers get fed up with it. It may be worth noting here that a visit by you to them, including travel time and expenses, may incur a considerable amount of money. Even to see people at the venue incurs a cost, and this should be borne in mind. Beware of inflating the number of contacts to people you like – or who make a good cup of coffee and are strategically situated between your office and home and available on Fridays at 3 p.m. – they may not need the additional contact, and time can then be better applied to other things. Beware too of putting off contact with ones you do not like, or who you know are likely to be difficult or who are geographically awkward; if they are good prospects, time must be allocated to them.

A balance in this area is clearly important, and it must be regularly reviewed; frequencies can and should change with changing circumstances. The greatest danger, though, is always going to be under-contact and losing touch.

Methods of contact

All possible methods should be considered and, almost always, a mix should make up the total list of contacts. A meeting, then a letter or a phone call keep the time and cost of some of the contacts low. What can you do? You can:

- *telephone:* this has immediate impact and, when contact goes well, it can contribute to the process positively. But it is difficult to choose your moment – they may be busy, distracted and there is no lasting element to the call on its own;
- *write:* a letter is personal, it can be retained, it can look good as well as containing a useful message. And it can link to a telephone call, a call being followed by a letter and vice versa;
- *send something:* a newsletter, a new brochure, a factsheet, notification of a change (of facilities, policy, price, etc.), an illustration or photograph, a copy of something such as a press release or a news story;
- *fax:* this comparatively new mode of communication combines a feeling of urgency with less formality than a letter (almost an 'external memo') – not to be overused, but useful;
- *visit:* you can call on them either by arrangement or unexpectedly (be careful how you use this last one);
- *invitation:* you can invite them to visit you, for a chat, for coffee, for a meal; or to another location such as your stand at an exhibition, another hotel in the group, head office, or somewhere and something that is unashamedly a treat – a function, show, a day at the races.

One more recent communications form, that of e-mail, is not ideally suited to sales follow-up. It is too easily ignored and deleted from both the system and the mind.

Such methods can, of course, work in a variety of combinations, and the possibilities of varying the way in which ongoing contact works are therefore considerable. What is best for an individual must be decided in light of their nature, and there will be some where contact is routine and not so frequent, others where the contacts must be much more carefully and individually worked out. There will also be times when contact must be increased in frequency, or made to have more impact if you are to achieve the objectives of the moment. However contact is made, the most important thing about it is the reason for making contact.

Reasons for contact

Consider first a typical scenario. A client has seen you, made some use of the hotel (apparently satisfactorily) and you now want to contact them with the view to exploring future possibilities. You telephone them. They are perfectly pleasant but say, in effect, '. . . nothing more at present . . .' What do you do next? After all, three more such contacts and the feeling is one of embarrassment. One way forward is always to ask when further contact may be appropriate. Will they talk again – at the end of the month, at the beginning of a new budget period, at the turn of the year, in three months? It is particularly useful to discover how their planning cycle works – 'We review such arrangements every year' – 'We start scheduling dates for the next period in April'. This approach may give you both your next date and a reason for contact. You can call and say to a secretary: 'I promised to call this week to . . .' But they are not always prepared or able to be this specific, and indeed you may feel contact is necessary before a major date such as the start of their new financial year.

So what then?

Too often what people do is very introspective. They want business and make contact with no other reason than that stated, I receive many calls that start: 'I was wondering if there are any other meetings we could accommodate . . .' and which say little more than 'We want some business.' Customers do not do business with you to help you, they make use of your property because it helps them. The best reasons for contact should always be stated in *customer* terms. If you telephone, ask yourself what the contact will do for them; when they put down the telephone will they say to themselves (or to a colleague) 'That was useful' or timely, and why.

What you need are often referred to as 'triggers' or 'hooks' around which you can hang the next contact. You should be able to think of many of these; indeed it may be worth keeping a list and noting which ones seem to prompt the best response. If you arrange ideas under some category headings then expand into and around these, you might well be surprised just how many you can list and thus use. For instance, be prompted by:

- *Your clients' internal arrangement*
  Culture or organizational change, accident, productivity moves, quality control problems or successes, employee morale, new appointments – again both crisis or success create opportunities.

Or it may be that the prompt is external:

- *Economic/political changes*
  Interest rates up/down, tax changes, exchange rate changes (making export more or less attractive), an election (always surrounded by a period of uncertainty), strikes, major legislative changes.
- *Seasonal*
  Any event or stage in the year will affect someone somehow: Christmas, New Year, Easter, school holidays, periods of high or low seasonal sales, seasonal weather (wet, dry, stormy, etc.).

Others may be more specific to the people involved in your clients/prospects:

- *Personal*
  Birthdays, anniversaries (e.g. wedding or a year in a new job), illness, retirement.

You can no doubt think of more and can personalize them to particular aspects of your business and individual clients. Some will work only for an individual; others may help you structure mini-mailings. Some are unexpected: for example in London as I write this a tragic IRA bomb outrage in the city of London has left office buildings uninhabitable and central hotels and meeting-places are offering alternative accommodation for meetings planned to be held internally. Others may affect only one client, but can be planned for. For example: you may know of someone's impending move to a new job in a different organization. This may prompt contacts that introduce you to his successor and follow him, if appropriate, to his new 'home'; such perhaps leads to two customers where there was only one.

Matching such triggers to those clients with whom you want to keep in touch, ringing the changes in terms of method, setting and maintaining the right frequency and always making the contact useful to the client will serve you well.

Special attention for major clients

Most people in selling are today aware of Pareto's Law (called after the Italian mathematician) or what is more usually called the 80/20 rule. This means that in most businesses 80 per cent of your revenue will come from 20 per cent of your customers. The figures will not, of course, be exact but some such percentage will apply. This emphasises the importance of the major clients; losing one can be a real problem (and having one or two who are disproportionally large can put you in a very vulnerable position); developing them effectively can be a real opportunity. In the hotel business it may apply especially to corporate business and may be more pronounced in some sectors of the business (e.g. banqueting) than others, but you should always remember that large customers are different in nature as well as scale. They need a different approach, may need more frequent contact, have more people to contact and no doubt demand keener prices on account of their size.

They may also need a more systematic and planned approach, the development of what some companies call a 'client strategy'. This involves analysis, and a plan being developed from that analysis, which will better develop the business across the range and throughout the client. What this analysis does is to take a matrix approach. Figure 6.2 (page 136) illustrates this, on a format which you can adopt or adapt to suit your approach. Essentially, this takes the different elements of the business on one axis, dividing into categories in whatever way your system allows – accommodation, restaurants, etc. – and the different 'markets', that is departments or people, to whom you do or might sell on the other.

Details of the customer, contacts and other details go at the top and the figures show:

P – potential, the total amount the client buys from everyone they deal with.

A – the actual revenue done in the last period quarter/year or whatever.

A *trend* column allows you to predict whether their future business is growing (or not) and, on the reverse, a target can be set for the coming period. The figure shows an example.

One of the most important things this shows about a large client is why it is large, where the business is coming from; if it is not coming equally from around the organization, then splitting it down like this will show gaps – and these may otherwise be missed or neglected within what is regarded as good results overall; the gaps flag opportunities and the plan begins to address how to tackle them.

The number of major accounts, very much the minority of the whole, keeps what has to be done here manageable. No one should say they have insufficient time to do this for their top ten or twenty (or whatever you decide) regular accounts. It is worth reviewing key accounts regularly in this way and discussing them with colleagues, or management, to make sure you arrive at the best way forward to handle them.

With the foregoing, even doing the analysis with estimated figures (almost 'on the back of an envelope') can show results. Another simple check to run on your larger clients is to keep a league table (see Figure 6.3, page 138). Just keeping a list in rank order period by period (it is shown by year, but could be less) will highlight the changes. Sometimes negative change is for positive reasons: a client may have dropped in position not because you are doing less business with them, but because other, perhaps new, clients are producing more. But again potentially it is a system that can prompt questions:

Compiled by: _____ Date: _____

Name and address: <u>XYZ Company</u>

Current contacts   R. Abuthnot   –   Company Secretary
                        F. Jones   –   Training Manager

Service/Market matrix covering period: _____

| | Markets | | | | |
	Mktg/ Sales	**Mnfctr**	**Training**	**Trend**	**Total**
Accomo-dation	P 20,000 A 7,000	2,000 1,000	12,000 4,000	Static	34,000 12,000
Food/drink	P 15,000 A 5,000	1,000 400	6,000 2,000	Static	22,000 7,400
Conferences	P 10,000 A 1,000	– –	4,000 –	Increase	14,000 1,000
Functions	P 1,000 A –	1,000 –	– –	Decl.	2,000 –
Incentives	P 5,000 A –	– –	– –	Increase	5,000 –
O'seas (scheme)	P 5,000 A –	1,000 –	– –	Increase (Export)	6,000 –
	P A				
	P A				
Trend	Increase. (esp. exp)	Static	Increase		
Total	P 56,000 A 13,000	5,000 1,400	22,000 6,000		

(Left margin vertical label: S E R V I C E S)

Competitive activity Company 'X' – strong – esp. in Marketing/Sales Department.

Figure 6.2: Customer strategy form example

| | **Markets** | | | |
	Mktg/ Sales	**Mnfctr**	**Training**	**Total**
Accomo- dation	18,5000	1,500	8,000	28,000
Food/drink	11,4000	600	4,000	16,000
Conferences	7,000	–	3,000	10,000
Functions	500	500	–	1,000
Incentives	2,000	–	–	2,000
O'seas (scheme)	2,500	500	–	3,000

Action:

Contacts to be made   Sales/Mgk Director and Co. Training Mgr.

Call frequency   Two pres. calls + four field sales force follow-up.

Objectives of calls   1. Create awareness of scheme.
2. Obtain detailed commitments/card orders.

Support required   1. Field force calls on Regional Sales Mgrs. re. their regular accommodation and conf. needs.
2. Presentations and entertainment from the General Manager to the Sales Director and Trg Manager (April), once outline company commitment received.

Figure 6.2: Customer strategy form example (continued)

| Customer | Turnover | | | | | | | | |
| | Last year | 2 years ago | | 3 years ago | | 4 years ago | | 5 years ago | |
	T/O	T/O	rank	T/O	rank	T/O	rank	T/O	rank
1									
2									
3									
4									
5									
6									
7									
8									
9									
10									
11									
12									
13									
14									
15									
16									
17									
18									
19									
20									
A Total £									
B Total company turnover £									
A/B %									

Figure 6.3: Major client league table

- Why is XYZ down?
- Have circumstances (people, experience of service, etc.) changed?
- Is something being missed?
- Can different action or approach in future increase the response?

Even a couple of good ideas from such a system turned into action can pay dividends in terms of extra sales. Regularly taking these sorts of view is likely to provide ongoing business opportunities.

Conclusions

Generally speaking, it is always easier to get more business from the people you know well and who know and approve the service they get from you, than it is to find new customers; though realistically both are always necessary. Continuity is important, you have to balance the tasks (and sometimes operational responsibilities as well) and this is sometimes difficult to achieve.

Never forget, however, the fickle nature of clients. Someone may stay with you regularly for many years and then receive a promotion from a new hotel, perhaps offering a trial deal which saves some money, and suddenly you see them no more (the likelihood of this can be compounded if they have minor complaints). No piece of business can be taken for granted, and sales action should be specifically designed to secure existing business and develop it in size, range and regularity.

7 | Making it work: the keys to success

I N THIS final short chapter I want to add some comments to highlight those things that contribute to getting the sales process right, that make the difference between getting an agreement or not. As has been said, there are no magic formulae. Selling is made to work first by an understanding of its many techniques, and a conscious effort (one that becomes a habit) to deploy them – individually and appropriately – on every occasion. Secondly, success stems from an attention to detail, ensuring that every technique, every nuance, every phrase and description, is deployed in exactly the way that will 'increase the danger of people doing business with us'.

Two perspectives are important here: that of the customer and that of those in the business. First, what do customers think? I took an informal straw poll of a number of people who use hotels extensively, mainly for corporate purposes, and found the following. This is not, of course, a scientific survey, but by any standards these were what most would surely regard as significant buyers, and there was considerable agreement amongst their views.

What clients say they want

'Above all I want someone who understands what I want – not just in terms of the many details – but who understands why things are important to me, and accepts that they are.'

'I like someone who takes trouble to find out and understand my point of view.'

'. . . someone who talks more about me and my requirements than about them, their property and its facilities.'

'Someone who is efficient, who has facts, literature and, if necessary, other people organized and ready to deliver what will help me make a sensible buying decision.'

'. . . and if they are wrong they admit their mistakes.'

'It is not a bit of good telling me the conference room holds 50 if it is quite clear that the top limit is, say, 35 . . . I want a true picture and I want promises kept 100 per cent.'

'If I do the tour of a place I want to feel that what I am shown and told is what I need to know and see and not the "standard pitch".'

'. . . and let me decide if and for how long I want entertaining, I am a busy man.'

'. . . a professional, who knows their stuff and respects me and my requirements.'

'What I really want is sound advice.'

'. . . I am after ideas as to how I can make best use of the facilities.'

'. . . if only they would talk less and listen more, much more.'

'I want to be *involved* in the show-round, not walking a yard behind, pulled along like a dog on a lead.'

The prevailing view that consistently came through (and many points were made in one way or another many times) is well catered for by the approaches discussed here; certainly the need for empathy and seeing things from the client's point of view is clearly crucial. It is also clear that 'seeing things from the client's point of view' is seen as understanding their specific use of a property, not just being 'nice to customers' in some general sense.

What about the negative side?

What clients do not like

'I don't like being taken for granted.'

'I just do not believe overstated claims, no property is able to cater for everything and right for anyone you care to name.'

'. . . they should not pretend they know it all.'

'I dislike any lack of respect, for me, my experience, my time.'

'They will only get the business if they are professional and that means concentrating on the business in hand. They should not assume I want to chat for hours.'

'. . . anyone who does not have the facts at their fingertips.'

'. . . they did not know basic facts about the place.'

'I was in a hurry and they could not even turn up on time.'

'I don't want to hear constant knocking of other places, I like and use some of the ones they were so disparaging about.'

'Above all, I hate being treated as if my proposed use of the hotel was that of just another customer – *my* requirements are *my* requirements and I regard them as unique.'

And I suspect such a list could run on – and on. There is certainly a moral here in terms of the attitude taken to customers. You need to make a very honest assessment of what your customers would say about you and your colleagues. Of course, there will be some negative points you know you are very definitely not guilty of, but there may be others where questions can be asked – and changes made.

Similarly, consider the positive points the things customers want; are they getting the right overall approach from you consistently, whenever and however and with whom contact takes place? Even the most aware establishments make errors or have blind spots. Sometimes this shows itself in small, though significant errors, just a phrase perhaps: I recently contacted a hotel, and was subsequently shown around by someone who told me only their name, not their job title. They handled things very well and I later recontacted the sales office to take things further, asking for them by name. 'Perhaps I can help you', said the person who answered the phone 'they (naming my previous contact) are only a trainee.' Maybe; but it was said dismissively – and anyway they had handled things very well. I do not like either people who are disloyal to colleagues or, if this is what they had done, being fobbed off with the 'office junior'. Either way it gave the wrong impression.

A good venue may well receive business despite such errors; but it will surely miss some. But sometimes the contact is obviously poor or uncaring; in this case business is much less likely to result. If errors of any sort, large or small, are to be avoided, you have to have constant feedback from customers and be very open to what they say. It is easy to see a good venue doing well and feel there must therefore be no room for improvement. To an extent the better the venue the easier this is. But for some, much of the business they do comes almost *despite* the standard of selling. Excellent facilities, first-class service or a convenient location will bring in business that does not need selling – the booking merely needs to be taken.

To rely on this, however, is very dangerous. Customers, as has been said, are fickle. And competition is ever active; business that comes to you virtually automatically, perhaps because you are the only provider of particular services in the area, may suddenly be in question when a competitor redevelops some of their services.

Selling must always be well deployed, and to make sure it is deployed effectively means being close to customers. Some of the feedback you need can be obtained through simple research; that is the questionnaires mentioned earlier. Realistically, much more comes through the normal ongoing contact with contacts and clients that occurs day by day. It is this which you must listen to carefully and be always open-minded about, never assuming that all is well but continuing to dig deeper to discover exactly how clients view the way they are dealt with.

What the industry thinks

To update on my feeling for the industry gathered over the time I have worked in it, I talked to a number of people in the industry just before handing the manuscript to the publishers – in London where I am based and in Singapore where I go regularly on business. What did they think made for sales effectiveness?

One point predominated. The conversation rate goes up dramatically for those prospects who visit the property. As Peter Hawley, General Manager of the Grand Hotel, Eastbourne (the hotel, incidentally that was voted 'Best UK Conference Hotel' in an industry award) said; 'By far the best way to sell a hotel is for the customer to view it.' Not so surprising perhaps, but it is useful. Certainly action geared to making a visit likely, and that simply directed vaguely at 'getting some business', are rather different. Aiming specifically for visits dictates the action and gives the whole sales effort greater certainty.

To quote further:

Telephone sales are vital and are often the first point of contact, but once a customer is on the premises the venue can speak for itself. Visits may take the form of specifically targeted appointments or a 'social' weekend with other buyers when soft selling can take place over two days.

In a face-to-face meeting a friendly but courteous

manner can win over the potential client and this engenders a feeling of trust to the buyer. Flexibility in terms of what the hotel can do for the client is of paramount importance. We must always strive to accommodate the client's wishes and this will further help the 'trusting' relationship.

Highlighting of unique selling points can be more persuasive than a continuous 'hard sell'. More and more people are aware of selling techniques and are on their guard against them. Straightforward honest talking can often lead to a quicker closing of the sale.

Fair comment; I would not disagree. As the appendix to Chapter 5 showed, however, there is showing round and showing round. The attractive venue does – to a degree – speak for itself and seeing it can, of itself, make a marked impression on a prospect. But if the conversation that accompanies this process shows a true understanding of the client and their needs, and the 'demonstration' element of the show-round is handled in the right kind of way, the overall effect is still more powerful. This, in my view, also goes some way towards countering the other point Peter Hawley makes about straightforward honest dealing as it does not seem like overt sales technique and indeed it is not – just 'helping people to buy'.

Another comment worth quoting comes from Paul Clayton, General Manager of Mottram Hall, a De Vere Group hotel, who said:

With the change in the economic climate many new sales ideas have come to fruition, although I do feel that the old, tried and tested sales techniques such as after-event call-backs, updating agencies with rates, mailshots and generally keeping in touch with clients, are the best techniques any salesperson can use.

We have now become more active in releasing the full potential of our clients and all staff must be 100 per cent committed to the sale and achieving targets and budgets. This needs positive thinking and energy to keep working at the business we have and ensuring that all staff are trained and motivated in our best sales technique, 'customer care' to ensure repeat business whether it be on the golf course, for leisure or for business.

The most influential factor for us has been the use of a good database to ensure we keep up-to-date with our clients using a relevant and up-to-date client base.

Everyone sums up in different words but the message seems to be similar:

- you have to be directing sales effort at the right people (hence the database);
- you have to handle the contact in the right kind of way (and the implication is that it needs some skill, hence Paul Clayton's comment about training – and this book!);
- you have to keep in touch and, in my view, do so in a way that is based on helping the client rather than, as can happen all too often, a sort of 'Anything you can throw my way at present' approach; and, in addition, all this has to be done in a way that is underpinned by suitable promotion.

Mailshots, for example, often designed to create opportunities and contacts for salespeople, have to be striking and say something of interest. Too often they are an introspective catalogue of facilities and features. You can sometimes substitute the property name and the top of the page or on the cover and no one would notice the difference. Whatever else they may do, one thing that is not on that list is 'differentiate'. This can be linked to a number of things: too small a budget; too much insular thinking. But it starts with organization and responsibility. Someone has to be responsible for co-ordinating the sales and promotional activity – sometimes they do not gel well only because they stem from two different departments and the left hand does not know what the right hand is up to.

A checklist approach

The former Hotel and Catering Training Board in the UK in the days of government-supported ITBs now operates as the Hotel and Catering Training Company. Much of their work is in what one might call the 'craft' areas, dealing for example with kitchen staff, but they overlap into management areas, and sales is a topic they deal with in various ways. From their detailed contacts with the industry they have put together a number of publications reflecting best practice, and selling crops up as an issue within the broader content of several others – and, with thanks for their permission to do so, I reproduce here three practical checklists from publications which they have produced.

These cover three key stages in the overall sales process:

1. making initial contact by telephone (Figure 7.1);
2. writing a good sales letter (Figure 7.2);
3. the face-to-face meeting (Figure 7.3).

The first two are from a publication called *Maximising Occupancy,* and the second is from another titled *Marketing for Hotels and Restaurants;* both are useful and can be obtained from the company's London office.

Who else is involved?

One useful comment made to me about how to improve sales technique was 'Let others do it for you.' The manager concerned was not advocating doing nothing; rather, on the basis of leaving no stone unturned, recommending that anyone who will sell for you should be well briefed and that time spent doing this was usually worthwhile.

Who are these other salespeople? Well, a number of other businesses have an interest in selling hotels; indeed, they make part of their living by so doing. These include travel agents, airline staff, people in airport kiosks and others who all sell with varying degrees of skill and expertise. On the one hand there are some of these – travel agents for instance – who tend towards the

- Set your objectives for the call: it might be to get the potential customer to visit you for lunch and see your function room. Do not be overambitious with your objective: it is very difficult to obtain a booking from just one telephone call.

- Make the call yourself. If you ask your secretary to do so, that will mean the person has to be kept holding on while the call is transferred, irritating in itself, and the person is likely to spend those moments wondering what the purpose of the call is going to be, and you will have additional resistance to break through.

- Have all the information in front of you, both about the prospective customer and the products that the person or company might require.

- Make sure that you will not be interrupted during the call.

- Smile when you talk. It may sound silly, but the smile is transmitted in the tone of your voice.

- Identify yourself by name, and also the name of your establishment. Don't rely on the person's secretary to have passed on your name.

- Use the person's name during the call.

- Take notes. Pencil and paper should always be at hand.

- Don't push if it is apparent that your call is unwelcome. Perhaps the prospect is busy at the time you call. Give a brief indication of why you are phoning – expressed as a benefit to the person – promise to ring back, and try to establish a time when it will be convenient to speak again.

- Keep the conversation as short as possible.

- Conclude the conversation by summarizing action agreed, and saying 'Thank you' or 'Goodbye'.

- Update your records, and follow up, for example by sending a brochure and a note to confirm arrangements for a meeting.

Figure 7.1: Making telephone sales calls

- Every letter should be individually typed – a simple job with a word processor, so if you don't have one, use a typing bureau or a freelance secretary who does. Photocopied letters always look impersonal.

- Address the recipient by name – Dear Mr Withers, Miss Lloyd, not Dear Sir or Madam; if you haven't got the names, try Dear Neighbour, or some other appropriate word.

- Use an eye-catching headline.

- Gain the reader's attention with the first twelve words or so.

- Keep the letter to one sheet unless there is a good reason for a longer letter.

- Appeal to the reader's curiosity by asking questions, linking to local events.

- Use lots of 'You's', and very few 'We's', 'I's' or 'They's'.

- Use short sentences, a maximum of 20 words in each. Where it will add impact, and reinforce what has been said in a previous paragraph or sentence, start sentences with 'And' or 'But'. The occasional sentence without a verb can also be effective. It is generally better to be a little too informal, rather than too formal. You are unlikely to use expressions like 'Thanking you in anticipation' in conversation, so avoid them in sales letters.

- A PS at the end of the letter will be read by most people, so is a useful way of drawing attention to your reply form, or mentioning a secondary selling point. A handwritten PS will stand out even more clearly.

- Emphasize one or two major selling points – the benefits to the customer.

- Say what is special about your offer, and who says so – but don't overpraise your products.

- Highlight your special menus, events, entertainment and so on, and refer to enclosures.

- Establish clearly what you want the reader to do: respond by telephoning, completing an attached reservation form —consider including something that will help you monitor the response, perhaps a voucher.

Figure 7.2: Writing a good sales letter

Planning
- know all you can about your targets and their needs;
- know your product;
- prepare your sales presentation;
- how will you demand attention, create interest, persuade and close?;
- know your bargaining range – prices, facilities, bookings.

Venue and timing
- most suitable for client – does he need to see your establishment? – is his time too valuable to visit you?
- be punctual;
- have all the information you may need with you.

Interview
- put yourself in his shoes;
- be relaxed and create the right image for your establishment;
- get his attention immediately by coming quickly to the purpose (it rarely pays to gossip);
- be sensitive to his mood and reactions;
- if you have not done so before find out his needs by asking him about his use of hotels and restaurants and his previous experiences;
- make the presentation (sales pitch) smartly but look for signals demanding explanations, discussion, change of course;
- look for hints of additional or changed requirements;
- answer any questions precisely if you don't know, promise to find out and contact him as soon as possible: this opportunity to show speed of service may be the key selling point;
- pace the meeting to his wishes as you proceed.

Close the sale
- it is easy to finish a meeting with a feeling of goodwill – but is this really all you wanted?
- ask for the sale – he is unlikely to make his mind up without your prompt;
- make a booking or, as a minimum, arrange a visit or telephone call for a further attempt;
- of course, if the situation does not look right it is better to conclude the meeting as quickly as possible but still attempt a positive lead for a further occasion.

Material
- visiting card and writing paper;
- appropriate brochures and detailed price lists;
- booking forms;
- photographs;
- list of clients;
- details of staff, details of bookings.

Figure 7.3: Face-to-face selling checklist

monosyllabic school of salesmanship: 'That's the flight booked, now can you help with a hotel? Where would you recommend?' They may suggest one but most often if you query it: 'Why that one?' they reply 'Well, it's on the list.' Sorry, of course they are not all like this (I have trained some!) but you should not rely on a first-class piece of salesmanship being conducted on your behalf.

Of course, it may well be the job of marketing to liaise with such intermediaries, to brief them (even to train them), but it may be useful for individual salespeople to liaise; you can find time to see the main travel agents who send you business. Certainly you should know how people who come to you via this route deal with things and how they speak of you and your property. You may have to build on this, and even correct basic errors or gaps in information. On the other hand, the best will be a source of information and you might find an informal lunch is a good way of swapping some ideas and helping each other. The hotel industry has a tendency to be rather incestuous, employing people who have exclusively a hotels background and then not encouraging very much in the way of searching for ideas externally to the industry. There is no monopoly on good ideas and while you may well feel there is little to be learned from someone selling market research or marmalade (though you might be surprised!), you should have feelers out a little more widely than just your nearest competitor. Every little helps in maximizing sales effectiveness.

An international dimension

Everywhere I have travelled, the challenge of selling hotels and venues seems to be essentially similar. Over time things do vary. Particularly, there is often a cycle of events in major cities: first growth creeps up on capacity, making some business easier to win, then new hotels open to cater for the additional demand and there is overcapacity. Selling then becomes more difficult and price is immediately under threat. This has happened several times over recent years in cities such as Singapore and Hong Kong. Other disparate external factors can influence the sales process, making it harder or less difficult by turns. The smog caused by fires raging in Indonesia during 1998/9 is one recent example of such unpredictable influence.

I have noticed that, perhaps not surprisingly, there is a tendency for the plushest hotels in the most sought-after locations to allow their sales approach to reflect what I have called allowing the place to speak for itself. This may be enough to impress some, first-time overseas visitors perhaps, but a local businessman looking for somewhere to hold his company's AGM or a regular place to put up visitors will take a much more hard-nosed view and needs selling in just the ways we have been reviewing.

So, some hotels may have certain natural advantages but, as the marketing director of one hotel in central Singapore said to me:

> We believe we are among the best hotels in the city, the region, perhaps the world. We have superb facilities, we offer excellent service, with style, and we are well located, but we still have to sell and sell hard. The international traveller is getting more experienced, more sophisticated and more demanding all the time. Local people are used to us, they expect the high standards and we are well aware there are choices – many of them and nearby – they want value for money and they want somewhere which accurately meets their needs and in which they have confidence that this will be the case. We must have first-class sales people, selling as effectively as possible; despite all our advantages, we can rely on nothing else to provide the business and profitability we need for the future.

If this is the case for a major and successful property, then it surely applies to everyone equally or more so. It seems to me very much the right way to think. Selling – the right kind of selling – is vital; let me now try to sum up something about the influences that should affect exactly how it is done if it is to be successful.

Conclusions

So, what is the consensus here? There are a number of elements we can perhaps pull together. Selling, as has been said, is dynamic. There is no one right way to go about it, and the old style 'selling by rote' is no longer appropriate, if it ever was. You have to constantly consider exactly how you should go about each meeting, and monitor your progress during the meeting to ensure you stay on track. In this book we have examined, in effect, three influences on what will prove most effective. The first provides useful clues but must be treated with great care.

The industry 'norm'

Perhaps the proviso should precede the advantages. The danger here is that 'the blind are leading the blind', that is one person looks at how another goes about things and copies it. That is fine if the standard is good and the approach effective. If, however, they are merely doing what was passed down to them from someone else, and in turn that methodology was given to them by . . . but you see the problem.

You must, of course, take advantage of what you see going on around you, amongst colleagues for instance, but you must do so critically. Always ask why something is done, or recommended to you to be done, in a particular way. And, if the answer amounts to no more than 'That's the system' or 'We've always done it like that', make sure you really feel it is appropriate before you adopt a similar methodology.

Further, it is worth specifically checking more widely to see what prevailing practices are actually used. Visit some of your competitors (stay at their properties too if your budget will cover the cost) and note what they do. Ask clients or contacts to show you brochures, sales letters or quotations received from other properties; the worst they can say is 'No', and while there will be some where such a question is inappropriate, there will be others where it poses no problem. It can be useful to call in occasionally and see a hotel further afield, perhaps as you travel – the fuller a picture you have of how things are done the better you can judge what techniques or approaches involved may help you. You must be careful not to overindulge in what might be seen as spying, but some research of this sort is undeniably useful.

Such investigation may stimulate a wealth of ideas. At one venue in the UK recently – a country venue – I was sent an audio tape of directions to play in the car to help me find it easily. Good idea, it worked well, and I asked who thought of it. 'Oh, we saw it being done somewhere else and copied it' was the reply. Well, it is nice to have original ideas, but realistically some come just this way, and why not?

The customer

Customers are the ultimate guide. Selling will never be effective if the way it is done does not satisfy the clients' service needs or if it is felt to be pushy, inefficient or just inappropriate or unprofessional. Make sure you get sufficient feedback from clients. I am often asked to fill in a questionnaire in the bedroom I have stayed in, or sent a form after using conference facilities. Such can certainly be useful, but they tend to concentrate on service, food, restaurants, etc. Surely it is just as important to know what people feel about earlier stages: how did they hear of you, how did they feel their enquiry was handled, what did they think of the way they were dealt with at the subsequent meeting? This kind of question can provide useful information; yet I have rarely seen such questions incorporated into these kinds of questionnaires.

Note: it is a small digression, but you should always acknowledge bad reports (no, people do not always do so); not only is it disproportionately annoying to the customer, but it may be an opportunity to turn the situation round and sell forward. Similarly you may want to respond to some others, the very flattering perhaps.

Every customer you see can increase your knowledge about and feel for what customers expect and what works best.

You

Whatever else, you have to do things your way. You cannot spend your every selling moment as an actor, attempting to be something you are not. You have to find your own way, an approach that suits and can be naturally deployed so that you and the customer are comfortable with what is going on. Certainly you can change your behaviour and acquire new habits (and perhaps lose old ones), resolving to ask more and better questions, or listen more. But, that done, you have to be yourself.

One thing you surely cannot fake, and that is enthusiasm.

An enthusiasm for your property and everything about it, and for your customers and their needs, will go a long way to helping you create the atmosphere and rapport you want. Again this is stimulated by seeing things from the customer's point of view. What may be a small piece of business for you, may be a very important arrangement for them. Treat it with the interest and enthusiasm *they* feel it deserves and they will like it; and *they* will remember too.

Enthusiasm is the one good thing in life that is contagious (that and laughter perhaps). Use it and you will create an added edge to your selling, something that the less aware competitor will miss.

Overall, a professional approach pays dividends. It does not guarantee success; nothing does that – and realistically you will not win them all – but it will make a good strike rate that much more likely. And, in a competitive business where the customers' final choice between alternatives is often finely balanced, it can just give you the edge that will swing the balance in your favour. The one asset you have to help you sell effectively that is available to no one else – is you. In a people business how can it be any other way?

Whatever else may have a bearing on creating success, three interlinked factors are clearly a knowledge of every detail of the property you sell, an understanding of the clients – each and every one individually – to whom you attempt to sell, and a belief in property, client and, perhaps above all in yourself. With that in mind I will leave the last word in this chapter to Jayne Burroughs (the Sales Manager at the UK conference centre Highgate House, who not only agreed to have one of her client meetings filmed for the Meetings Industry Association film *Comprehending Clients*, mentioned on page 23, but made such a good job of the meeting despite a clutch of cameras and technicians hovering two feet behind her shoulder). Asked to summarize her views on what makes for a successful approach, she said:

> Selling a conference for twenty delegates seated theatre-style with private dining is entirely different from selling a packet of mints . . . or is it?
>
> The basic approach principle is the same, the need to attract the client's interest and desire in order to encourage the client to buy.
>
> Selling techniques are also similar, setting objectives, questioning techniques, overcoming objections, and ultimately that all-important closing of the sale.
>
> It is a combination of the aforementioned techniques together with an abundance of enthusiasm from the salesperson presenting a venue that they truly believe in, plus that all-important product knowledge, which instills confidence in the client and proves most successful.

8 | Afterword

'He that will not apply new remedies must expect new evils; for time is the greatest innovator.'

Francis Bacon, 1625

The emphasis of this book has been on techniques, on what should be done and just how these techniques should be deployed to ensure the greatest chance of sales success. If any review of this sort is to be useful in the long term, then the ways of going about things that it commends must be implemented appropriately by individual salespeople in light of the precise sales job they do.

In addition, the dynamic nature of the sales process has been stressed. There is no one 'right' way to sell hotels, or anything else for that matter. What matters is that the techniques are deployed, as has been said, client by client, day by day, meeting by meeting. Only in this way can approaches be kept up-to-date and can it be ensured that the best approach is always deployed for each and every client situation. The essence of the process is one of 'fine-tuning' skills. Because of the need for constant review and change, you need a coach. And, while you may get or seek assistance from managers, colleagues and others, the only coach who is always available – is yourself.

Consider a different situation. You are, let us suppose, keen on some sport: tennis or golf, perhaps. In a fit of financial recklessness, and a good commission payment this month, maybe, you book some lessons with the coach or professional at the local club, in the hope of improving your game. A poor tennis coach will usually start by getting you to play for a few minutes and observing what you do. Then they will pause and tell you *all* the things you are doing wrong. They mention your grip on the racket, your stance, etc. 'Now, have another go' they conclude, brightly. So, attempting to concentrate simultaneously on all the specific points made, you have another go. What happens? You are lucky if you can get the ball over the net at all. Your game gets worse. Concentrating on so much at the same time just does not work.

The good coach, on the other hand, will mention one thing specifically. 'Maybe there are a number of things we can work on – let's look at the grip first and see if we can improve that.' You do; and it does. The same principles of improvement work elsewhere, and they work with selling.

Do not go to your next meeting and try to think consciously about everything you have read: there are too many variables. Review one or two things. Better still, make a list of those areas where you think there is 'fine-tuning' to be done, and review them progressively over a number of meetings. You are the best coach you have got, certainly the only one who is always there. By all means take advice, information and experience from anyone and anywhere, and at least think about it. What you deploy, and how, is your decision. Develop the habit of review, and fine-tuning will become a habit; you will constantly – regularly – be making small changes, improvements, to the detail of what you do. Then sales success – or at least an above-average success rate – can become a habit too.

The following summarizes those key elements of the sales process which, I believe – and experience shows – are most likely to help you differentiate what you do from what competitors do – to give you an edge in the marketplace. These particularly should be the basis of the kind of personal review advocated above; you may wish to add or subtract from this and must decide your own priorities.

- *Planning:* you must be organized, see the right people, the right number of people, on the right frequency and manage the sales process.
- *Preparation:* there must simply be no such thing as an

unplanned contact, and whether preparation takes two minutes or two hours, it must always happen.

- *Understand the structure:* you will do better at every stage if you have a clear idea of what should be going on overall.
- *Manner:* salespeople are not universally welcomed; the right manner will help put you in the ranks of the professionals.
- *Direction:* get hold of the meeting; run the kind of meetings you want and customers find they like.
- *Identifying needs:* find out more clearly, thoroughly and precisely what prospects want and why, and everything thereafter will be less difficult.
- *Listening:* this is vital for identifying needs, obtaining information and part of the image that needs projecting.
- *Clarity:* nobody buys what they feel they are inadequately informed about; everybody appreciates clear guidance on something they anticipate being complex.
- *Talk benefits:* it focuses what is done on the customer and makes it more descriptive in their terms.
- *Handling objections:* do it confidently and realistically and you build your image as a professional.
- *Closing:* if you cannot close you will never sell effectively.
- *Write persuasively:* be as persuasive on paper as when face-to-face; do not let this be a weak link.
- *Formal presentation:* sell as effectively 'on your feet' to a group as across the desk; more and more customer situations demand it.
- *Persistence:* maintain contact, chase for a conclusion, do not allow paranoia to affect you.

In addition, you must:

- use the hotel, or whatever venue you sell, to make a case (do not assume it speaks for itself and all you have to do is show it to prospects – your competitors no doubt have good things to show also);
- link the whole process to customer needs (remember you are not simply selling facilities, but helping customers make their stopover, stay, meeting, break – whatever they need –

successful) and do so with a healthy measure of *adaptability* – so that you think about what you do, regard it as dynamic and changing, never believe in one 'right' way or get in a rut in which you operate on 'automatic pilot' rather than conscious of what exactly you are up to; only deploy techniques as appropriate to individual clients and have the confidence to succeed.

If you adopt a thoughtful and professional approach to your task, then everything you do can play a part in differentiating your property from others and increasing the likelihood of people saying 'Yes' more often than they say 'No'. Regard this book as a start to an on-going process of self-evaluation (asking yourself the kind of questions listed in the final Figure 8.1, a contact evaluation form), something you do by way of analysis after all or most of your contacts, and continuous adjustment and improvement will become a habit.

In this way you can improve your success rate immediately and develop it further in the future; a future you can be sure will in all probability be even more competitive to sell in than the present. So, everything you do matters, and every good decision about how you do things will help.

As Voltaire said: 'God is on the side not of the big battalions, but of the best shots.'

Objectives _____	Date _____
_____	Salesperson _____
_____	Customer _____

Selling activity	Yes	No	Comments/Action
1 *Pre-calling planning* Did you have specific objective for call?			
Did you prepare information?			
Did you have a call plan?			
Did you have sales aids planned and checked?			
2 *Opening interview* Did you gain attention?			
Did you explore needs?			
Did you get customer talking?			
About your needs?			
3 *Sales presentation* Did you use visual aids?			
Did you match benefits to customer needs?			
Did you anticipate objections?			
Did you get customer involved?			
Did you use simple language?			
4 *Handling objections* Did you recognize objections?			
Did you handle them satisfactorily?			
Did customer accept the answers?			
5 *Close* Did you ask test questions?			
Did you recognize buying signals?			
Did you ask customer for booking?			
Did customer book?			

Figure 8.1: Contact evaluation form

Index